Who Are You, My Daughter?

Ellen F. Davis
All Saints' Day 2003

And Ruth the Moabite said . . . , "So, I'm going to go to the field and glean."
(Ruth 2:2)

Who Are You, My Daughter?

Reading Ruth through Image and Text

Ellen F. Davis
Translation and Notes

Margaret Adams Parker
Woodcuts

Westminster John Knox Press
LOUISVILLE • LONDON

Book design by Margaret Adams Parker
Typesetting by PerfecType, Nashville, Tennessee
Cover design by Night & Day Design
Cover illustration: Margaret Adams Parker

First edition
Published by Westminster John Knox Press
Louisville, Kentucky

This book is printed on acid-free paper that meets the American National Standards Institute Z39.48 standard. ♾

PRINTED IN THE UNITED STATES OF AMERICA

03 04 05 06 07 08 09 10 11 12 — 10 9 8 7 6 5 4 3 2 1

Library of Congress Cataloging-in-Publication Data

Davis, Ellen F.
    Who are you, my daughter? : reading Ruth through image and text / Ellen F. Davis, translation and notes; Margaret Adams Parker, woodcuts.— 1st ed.
      p. cm.
    Includes bibliographical references.
    1. Bible. O.T. Ruth—Criticism, interpretation, etc. I. Bible. O.T. Ruth. English. Davis. 2003. II. Title.
    BS1315.52 .D38 2003
    222'.3506—dc21

                                    2002027028

for Margaret and Michael

and

for Gillian and Steve
in celebration of their marriages

Let us celebrate your love more than wine.
(Song of Songs 1:4)

Contents

Illustrations

Translator's Preface

*T*his annotated and illustrated translation of the book of Ruth functions much like a clock with a glass face, whose working parts are visible behind the hands: you cannot look at it without being aware, to some degree, of how it works. Similarly, this book aims at being transparent to the inner workings of one small book of the Bible. Its ultimate goal is to give "viewers"—for our version of Ruth is designed to be seen as well as heard—an expanded understanding of the processes of reading and interpreting a biblical book. How does a biblical book invite interpretation and offer guidance to its interpreters, yet do so without dictating a single "correct" reading? What choices does a translator or an illustrator make, and what other possibilities are hidden once those choices are made? By pointing to questions such as these, we offer this rendering of Ruth in words and images as one example of how the Bible may be viewed with fresh interest and genuine curiosity.

Why curiosity, a virtue not frequently associated with reading the Bible? Because the biblical writers are at every point urging us to a more probing and wonder-filled way of thinking about things we take for granted when we encounter them in our lives, things we read right past when we find them on the pages of Scripture. It is not only or primarily through tales of the supernatural that the writers engender wonder. (There is, in fact, not a single supernatural moment in the book of Ruth, and such moments are rarer in the Bible as a whole than we generally suppose.) Much more often, the writers evoke more or less ordinary aspects of human existence in ways that reveal them to be opportunities for self-transcendence and therefore potential points of contact with God. It is the peculiar vocation of those who serve Israel's God to speak and act in ways that make God's character more evident, inviting God's blessing, God's action-for-good, into their lives. The book of Ruth is about a small group of people who have unusual success in that vocation. So this is one good place to enter into the Bible and attempt to view it in a new way.

Perhaps the most important thing to be said about this translation is that it sounds like one. That is a matter of deliberate choice, but it should be acknowledged that my choice runs counter to another good principle of translation, currently more popular: "Any translation is a good one in proportion as you can forget, while reading it, that it is a translation at all" (Knox, *On Englishing the Bible*, 94). So the best translation of Ruth would sound as if the story had been written by a native English speaker. For the record, I am not a translational purist; if I were producing a translation for use in public worship, I would for the most part want people to forget that they were hearing a translation. In other words, I would want them to hear themselves being immediately addressed by the Scripture reading. However, there is no such thing as an all-purpose translation of the Bible. The present one is not written for large public readings. Rather, it is intended for people who are willing to take the time to dwell on a text that is partially foreign to them, to ponder the implications of curious word choices, to follow a trail marked by the repetition of key words—that most distinctive feature of biblical style that is generally muted, and often obliterated altogether, by translations. In a word, it is intended for study, so that its readers may begin to understand how the biblical writers habitually make meaning.

Sometimes, I admit, the word choices here sound more curious in English than they do in Hebrew—but where this is so, my aim is to preserve an effect of the Hebrew that would otherwise be lost. The outstanding example here would be the word *kallah*, which appears immediately and recurrently: four times in the first chapter. It designates Naomi's relationship to Orpah and Ruth; it is the ordinary Hebrew word for "daughter-in-law." Yet something is lost by translating it thus in English, for it is also the ordinary Hebrew word for "bride." "Daughter-in-law" is for English speakers a perfunctory statement of relationship, sometimes with negative associations. "Bride" is a word that connotes joy, hope, expectation, perhaps trepidation. There is a special poignancy in its frequent appearance in the first chapter of Ruth, which begins with the deaths of three husbands. Therefore, I have chosen to translate it "bride-daughters," even though that entails creating an English neologism out of a word that belongs to the standard vocabulary of the biblical writers.

This translation differs from most others in that I aim at verbal consistency. That is, a given Hebrew word is almost always rendered with the same or similar English wording in each of its occurrences. Repetition of certain words—generally nouns and verbs—is an important means whereby the biblical writers develop their central themes and also establish connections among events that would otherwise appear to be unrelated. It may seem unlikely to us that an audience would be expected to remember how a word has been used earlier and to draw connections on that basis between two scenes. Yet it should be remembered that the culture of ancient Israel was primarily aural. Even though some Israelites were composing sophisticated written literature as early as the tenth century B.C.E., throughout the biblical period most people would have heard rather than read stories and other literary works. Therefore, popular attention and memory were fixed by memorable words. Sadly, the closest analogue in our culture would be the way popular memory is keyed to the repeated images and accompanying slogans of commercial advertising.

Because we are not accustomed to listening carefully to sophisticated literature—and the book of Ruth is a finely crafted, though short, literary work—word repetition sounds awkward to us, and "good" English style does not favor it. Moreover, a given Hebrew word almost certainly has a different range of usage than its nearest English equivalent, so the most "natural" translational choice is to use different words in different situations. For instance, I know of no other translation of Ruth that follows the Hebrew in using the same word to express Ruth's repeated action of "sticking" (*davaq*). First she "stuck by" Naomi (1:14, commonly rendered "clung to"); later, Boaz and Naomi advise her pointedly to "stick with" Boaz's female field-workers (2:8, 21, 23)—and not with the males. The verbal repetition draws a line connecting Ruth's initial protective action toward Naomi on the road back to Bethlehem with the reciprocal concern of these elders for her, a young stranger in the land who is perhaps more vulnerable than she perceives herself to be.

The repeated word that above all others serves to focus the message of the book of Ruth is *ḥesed*, which I translate "good-faith" (1:8) or "act-of-good-faith" (3:10). *Ḥesed* is a quality that human beings share with God. It is that generous ability to put the interests of another, weaker, party before one's own. As such, it is the quality that Israel, uniquely in the ancient world, perceived to be characteristic of its God YHWH (on the divine Name, see the note at 1:6), "a God merciful and gracious, of long patience and abounding in *ḥesed* and faithfulness" (Exod. 34:6). Reciprocally, Israel understood God's requirement that *ḥesed*, toward one another and toward God, be characteristic of humanity:

> He has told you, humanity, what is good,
>   and what YHWH seeks from you:
> nothing but doing what is right, and loving *ḥesed*,
>   and walking humbly with your God.
>
>   (Mic. 6:8)

From a biblical perspective, the moral ecology of the world functions properly when God and humanity are engaged in the perpetual exchange of *ḥesed*, good-faith and the acts that follow from it. The very first words spoken in the book of Ruth seek the realization of that ideal: "And Naomi said to her two bride-daughters, 'Go, turn back, each woman to the house of her mother. May YHWH do good-faith with you, just as you have done with the dead and with me'" (1:8).

The book of Ruth as a whole gives the virtue of *ḥesed* narrative form and substance, and probably that is the reason for the book's extraordinary appeal. If indeed it is "one of the best books in the Bible," that is not only, as the eighteenth-century political essayist Thomas Paine wryly observed, because "it is free from murder and rapine" (Thomas Paine, *The Age of Reason*, cited in Sasson, *Ruth*, 196). More than for what is absent, Ruth is beloved for what is there, namely, a story of remarkable transformation: emptiness turning to abundance, desolation and isolation yielding, under the gentle and steady pressure of *ḥesed*, to new life in family and community. Yet Ruth is a realistic story, not a fairy tale. Which is to say, the action of the characters is imitable, repeatable, and that is why Ruth *should* appeal to us, as Jews and Christians who believe that Scripture offers basic guidance for fruitful living. So it is important to note at the outset that, while all three main characters are remarkable persons, they do not practice virtue solely as individuals. They also belong to a social system that makes legal provision for the dignity and the material needs of its weaker members:

widows, strangers, the poor. So Torah regulations of gleaning and land redemption are part of the essential background against which this story occurs. Certainly, the biblical writers intend for us to see in Ruth one memorable example of living by the teachings of Torah, of which it is said, "If humanity does them, it will live through them" (Lev. 18:5).

The three components of this book—translation, notes, and images—were from the outset conceived as complementary elements of a single project. The medium of woodcut is an excellent stylistic match for the story, which has the aura of a folktale, artfully yet simply told. But there is also a difference among the several elements. Whereas the translation and the images are confined to a single interpretive choice for each moment or phrase, the notes are designed to explain what may not be self-evident and also to raise questions, to disclose ambiguities and roads not taken (this time) by translator and illustrator.

Whatever may be distinctive about this rendering of Ruth is due to the fact that neither text nor image has at any time enjoyed precedence as an interpretation of the biblical text. Margaret Adams Parker and I seesawed back and forth as we examined each scene of the biblical story, each influencing and reshaping the other's view of it. It has been slow work, as true collaboration always is, and maybe that is its greatest value for study of the Bible. For the Bible, as its best interpreters in every age have known, yields its riches only gradually, to those who are patient with detail. If two minds are indeed better than one, it is because in tandem they grind more slowly.

A NOTE ON THE TRANSLATION

I have assigned titles to each of the four chapters of Ruth. Although these are not found in the Bible itself, they reflect the dominant theme of each chapter. All biblical translations, including those in the notes, are my own.

Artist's Preface

The painter Henri Matisse commented on the effort—"something very like courage"—that the artist must exert in order to "see everything as it really is." He cautioned that the simplest subject can be the most difficult: before the artist can paint a rose, "he has to forget all the roses that were ever painted," setting aside that "flood of . . . images which are to the eye what the prejudices are to the mind" (Matisse, "Looking at Life with the Eyes of a Child," 148).

Matisse's words also seem appropriate to my task of illustrating a beloved tale from Scripture. When a story is as familiar as Ruth, or Noah and the ark, or David and Goliath, we (artist and reader alike) come to the text "knowing" the story already. And we often know what it looks like as well, our responses preconditioned by the cheerful and brightly colored images from children's storybooks and Bibles. How many of us carry in our imaginations an image of Ruth: young, willowy, and beautiful? Or the tenderness of the moment when Ruth declares her loyalty to Naomi? In the face of those known and long-accepted images, how difficult it can be to summon the curiosity toward the text that Ellen Davis envisions in her Translator's Preface.

So our challenge has been to explore the text, in Matisse's phrase, "as it really is." Our readers will note immediately that we think the story is *not* the conventional romantic idyll depicted by many illustrators. The story contains elements that we recognize more readily from the nightly news than from the stock romantic tale: refugees and widows, the broken and the destitute, the foreigner. The tale is more correctly understood as one of suffering and loss redeemed by steadfast faithfulness. And while the story ends on a note of tender joy and hope for the future, it is neither carefree nor light.

In what ways did this understanding of the story shape the woodcuts? What other factors informed the images? Ellen Davis notes that the illustrations are "confined to a single interpretive choice." The decisions and changes made in the process of reaching these final images are hidden, but they are nevertheless significant to the goals of our joint commentary. I offer an overview of them here, in hopes of making "transparent" the workings of a biblical commentary created in visual form.

My first decision was to create the images as woodcut prints. Since woodcut is my primary medium as a printmaker, this was a choice made without much deliberation. In retrospect, it seems particularly apt. Woodcut is among the simplest and most direct of printmaking techniques: I simply carve away the areas that I want to remain white, roll ink onto the block, and, by rubbing, transfer the image to the paper. In this most basic form, the woodcut image is limited to black and white; the medium is thus characterized by sobriety, even starkness of expression. These qualities make it suitable for our reading of Ruth as a dramatically serious tale where the marks of suffering and hardship are never completely erased.

The decision to create a "running narrative" of images also came early and was extraordinarily important. A scene-by-scene exploration of a story mandates a closer reading of the text than is necessary when one image serves to summarize the meaning of the whole. I learned this near the beginning of the project, when I began picturing Ruth's famous declaration of loyalty to Naomi. I was confident that I understood this scene, which I had already depicted twice in sculpted form. In each case I had shown it as a moment of tenderness, representative of the totality of the relationship between Ruth and Naomi. But as Ellen Davis points out in her notes, careful reading of that particular moment in the text reveals tension, even exasperation, and the woodcut I eventually created reflects that understanding.

Creating a running narrative also required that I pay attention both to the overarching trajectory of the tale and to the internal consistency of the individual parts. The story moves from desolation to gladness, from emptiness to fulfillment; each scene must fit into that gradual but all-encompassing transformation. So when we first see Naomi, she is bereft of husband and sons. Her head is bowed, and she clasps her arm across her breast as though closing herself off from the world and from any hope of comfort. In our final glimpse, her head is bowed once again, but her arms have been filled; she is looking down tenderly at a child in her embrace. In addition to these larger thematic concerns, I had to address the more practical considerations of consistency in dress and appearance. It was particularly interesting, as the project neared completion, to examine the entire set of images, searching for inconsistencies. Was there a logic to the dress? Ruth moves from widow's black to festive garments, while Naomi does not. Was there consistency in appearance? Once I had decided to depict Ruth as taller than Naomi, she needed to remain so throughout the narrative. Ruth's hair must always be curly, and Boaz's beard, graying.

Interestingly, as I worked on the images, each character began to take on dimensions and characteristics that illuminated my understanding of the story. These characteristics were carried as much by gesture as by facial expression. (Artists are aware that the body "tells" a person's story; a minute shift in the angle of shoulder or chin can lift a character from despair into hope.) For instance, when Naomi takes the initiative, sending Ruth out to encounter Boaz on the threshing floor, her whole stance is different, more open and confident than before. With the depictions of Boaz, gesture is particularly significant in revealing character. The text describes both Boaz and Ruth as "valorous" (in character rather than martial prowess), underscoring the appropriateness of the match between them. Boaz and Ruth are fit partners, equals. So I picture Boaz, in the first meeting with Ruth in the fields, crouching down as he speaks with her. We might have expected him to stand or to bend over the kneeling woman. It is a measure of his character (and a significant and unusually egalitarian gesture in a culture that subordinated women) that he instead lowers himself to speak with her.

Of the three central characters, Ruth departs most markedly from conventional representations. I show her determined and strong. In her demeanor toward others, there is a grace that reveals her innate kindness. She is attractive rather than beautiful. And although still young, she does not appear youthful. While this picture may run counter to the image we retain from the illustrated volumes of our childhood, we might do well to recall the strong-boned women we see on the evening news, women carrying babies at their hips and possessions on their heads. Any one of them might tell a tale like Ruth's, and like the young widow who leaves her own country and then heads out daily to work in the sun-scorched fields, they are past their youthful beauty. But Ruth's hands are her most striking feature. They are large and capable and highly expressive. We see her work with her hands, eat with them, carry burdens with them, and above all, talk with them. This emphasis results in part from my own fascination with hands and from their importance in my work as printmaker and as sculptor. But by happy chance the prominence of Ruth's hands parallels the text's allusions to the Woman of Valor from Proverbs 31:10–31. As Ellen Davis has pointed out in her commentary on Proverbs, that woman's hands are her outstanding physical feature, and the poet draws repeated attention to their activities (Davis, *Proverbs, Ecclesiastes, and the Song of Songs,* 153). Surely it is fitting that "our" woman of valor should have hands equally remarkable.

The community of men and the community of women constitute two additional visual presences, paralleling their significance in the text. Men and women remain in distinct groups, even on those rare occasions when they are seen together. But they form a kind of alternating chorus that comments on events in the story. As Naomi returns to Bethlehem, the women are seen to murmur to one another in astonishment, "Is this Naomi?" Later the men gather at the gate, witnesses to the bargaining scene between Boaz and P'loni Almoni. And at the end the women gather to attend the childbirth, blessing the Lord and giving the baby a name.

Not surprisingly, one of the most difficult challenges was finding a way to convey the abstract. How might I represent Ruth's identification as a foreigner or P'loni Almoni's anonymity? How could I create a visual link between Ruth's story and David's genealogy, with which the book concludes? Ruth's foreignness is, of course, crucial in the story. The text identifies her repeatedly as "the Moabite." I decided to set her apart from the Israelite women by giving her a tattoo on her forehead. Since tattoos are forbidden to Jews under rabbinic law, this visual device is eminently appropriate. In the case of P'loni Almoni, a character who is not dignified with a real name, I picture him from behind: nameless in the text, he is faceless in the illustration. Finally, the illustration for the genealogy of David connects him visually with his ancestor Boaz. I show him with the same features (but without gray in his hair), clasping his hands in the way that is characteristic of Boaz throughout the woodcuts.

In the end, the single most important factor in the creation of these images was my intention to create a commentary in visual form. This meant that every decision and change, quite literally, moved the images in the direction of greater historical accuracy or fidelity to the text. The most striking example of this occurred as I worked on the opening image of Elimelekh and his family fleeing into Moab. Refugees are a recurring theme in my work, and I had envisioned this family as a generic group of refugees, headed off across an expanse of open desert under a blazing sun. But when Ellen Davis discovered early-twentieth-century photographs of the actual route into Moab (in modern-day Jordan), I redrew the scene and showed the family staring into that formidable pass through the mountains (Elmendorf, *A Camera Crusade through the Holy Land*, plate 21).

Partway through this project, I became aware of biblical scholar Brevard Childs's "Criteria for Evaluating a Commentary's Excellence." In his list of suggestions, Childs urges the commentator to "lead the reader back to the biblical text," to "deal seriously with the profoundest dimension of the biblical text," and never to allow a "private agenda to overshadow the text itself" (Childs, "The Genre of Biblical Commentary as Problem and Challenge," 192). I find these admonitions particularly moving, since they very aptly describe my own goals when picturing Scripture. Moreover, the parallels serve to confirm my belief that the visual image can be a form of biblical commentary that is both valid and significant.

Acknowledgments

This project, first conceived as a set of woodcuts, has emerged as a book that uses both text and image to render the biblical narrative vivid to the contemporary reader. Several people have been instrumental in the process: Dwayne Huebner first suggested the collaboration, Bruce Parker prepared the blocks for the first woodcuts, Margaret Jones solved the most complex problems of design, Judith Winshel provided a critique of the woodcuts, and Carol Shoun edited the manuscript. Stephanie Egnotovich, our editor, believed in the project and made it possible. We especially thank students from the Virginia Theological Seminary and Duke Divinity School; many of their ideas are represented in the translation and the notes.

This book began in celebration of the wedding of one daughter and concludes with the wedding of another. We offer it to them and their husbands with our love.

Who Are You, My Daughter?

CHAPTER ONE

Turning Back

1   *And it happened, in the days of the judges' judging, that there was a famine in the land. And a man went from Bethlehem Judah to sojourn in the fields of Moab — he, and his wife, and his two sons.*

2   *And the name of the man was Elimelekh ("My-God-is-king"), and the name of his wife, Naomi ("My-pleasantness"), and the names of his two sons, Maḥlon ("Sickness") and Kilyon ("End-of-the-line") — Ephratites from Bethlehem Judah. And they came to the fields of Moab, and there they were.*

1:1 *the judges' judging*—In the period before the rise of the monarchy, Israel was a kinship-based society. The extended family was the basic unit of social and economic organization, a fact that is crucial to this story. Because of their important role as economic producers, Israelite women seem to have exercised more social power in the subsistence-level economy of this period than they would in the more stratified society of the monarchic period. That the very first phrase evokes this early period is no coincidence. The author, writing probably in the time of the monarchy, lifts up the story of two powerful women who lived in a time when women's actions were a strong force in shaping the identity of a people still in its (collective) youth.

Bethlehem Judah—Bethlehem, "House-of-Bread," is so named because in ancient times it served as the "breadbasket" for nearby Jerusalem. Bethlehem occupies a small plain in the southern hill country. (The designation "Judah" distinguishes it from the town of the same name in the northern region of Galilee.) To this day it remains the most suitable place for growing grain in the vicinity of the capital city. The story begins with an ironic reversal of expectations, for it seems that now the pagan land of Moab (in modern Jordan) is more fertile than the promised land of Israel, with its House-of-Bread. This is the first of many reversals of expectation and situation in this story, in which the "ordinary" upheavals that affect and periodically devastate every human life are seen to be occasions for the operation of God's grace and also of human kindness.

1:2 This family story is of national importance, since it tells of the ancestors of King David, yet it is marked by some of the imaginative and amusing characteristics of a folktale. One of these is the fact that the names of most of the characters are descriptive. They generally function either to establish a theme or to say something about the character's role in the story. Elimelekh's name, "My-God-is-king," is in the former category. Elimelekh has no role at all except to die and leave his family without husband and father. In a society in which all legal rights resided in the institution of the "father's house" and the adult males were the publicly recognized representatives of the household, such a situation would have been painfully vulnerable. So Elimelekh is important in this story chiefly for his absence. Yet in his very absence, his name stands as a reminder that there is another source of protection for this family—less obvious, but ultimately reliable—namely, the God who is sovereign over all the circumstances of human lives.

Maḥlon . . . Kilyon—These names appear nowhere else in the Old Testament, and they are unenviable. They bespeak the destiny of those who bear them: Naomi's sons will sicken and die, young and without issue.

Ephratites—In Genesis, Bethlehem is also known as "Ephrat(ah)" (Gen. 35:16, 19; 48:7). Perhaps this is the old name of the clans of the region, and the designation emphasizes the ancestral ties that connect these refugees to the home they now leave behind.

and there they were—The phrase is unusually blunt, in Hebrew as well as in English. The storyteller's intent may be to make us sense that the family's situation is badly compromised, even before tragedy strikes. The midrash (the compilation of medieval rabbinic commentary on the book) criticizes Elimelekh sharply for leaving the land of Israel. The rabbis supposed more than the text actually says: that he was a rich man who chose to look out for himself rather than help his neighbors in a desperate time. So the early deaths of Elimelekh and his sons were viewed as punishment for the great sin of leaving the God-given land of Israel.

"There they were," living as sojourners in Moab, a place that from an Israelite perspective was definitely on the wrong side of the tracks—that is, the wrong side of the Jordan. The Israelites told an unflattering story that the Moabites were descended from the incestuous union of Lot and his daughter (Gen. 19:37), which followed the destruction of Sodom and Gomorrah. In more recent memory, on the very verge of entering the promised land, the Israelites "whored after" Moabite women and made sacrifices to their god, Baal Peor ("Lord of Peor," Num. 25), with disastrous consequences. In short, to the ancient Israelite mind, Moab represented the quintessence of perversion and godlessness. This was an unpromising place for an Israelite family with two young sons to settle.

And a man went . . . to sojourn in the fields of Moab.
(Ruth 1:1)

3   *And Elimelekh died—Naomi's husband—and she was left, she and her two sons.*

4   *And they took for themselves wives, Moabites. The name of the one was Orpah ("Back-of-the-neck"), and the name of the second, Ruth. And they settled there for about ten years.*

1:3   *her two sons*—Subtly, the storyteller underscores Naomi's desolation, the loss of the "pleasantness" that her very name implies: "His" sons (vv. 1, 2) are now "hers" alone.

1:4   *wives, Moabites*—The first sentence hints at a small drama. The last two words in the sentence might also be translated by the more ordinary phrase "Moabite wives." In contrast to English, Hebrew word order places adjectives *after* the nouns they modify, so we have to wait until the end of the sentence to know what kind of wives the young men actually took. (We might imagine that there were other Israelite refugees in Moab, among whom they might have found conventionally suitable wives.) Intermarriage with foreigners was expressly forbidden in Torah (Exod. 34:16; Deut. 7:3), and the prohibition on Moabite alliances was the most stringent of all. In Moses' farewell address, the teaching is explicitly given: "No Ammonite or Moabite shall come into the congregation of YHWH, even to the tenth generation. . . . Because they did not meet you with food and water on your way out of Egypt, and against you they hired Balaam . . . to curse you" (Deut. 23:4–5 Heb. [3–4 Eng.]). Centuries after "the days of the judges' judging" (approximately the twelfth and eleventh centuries B.C.E.), that prohibition would not be wholly forgotten. Nehemiah, the fifth-century community organizer who built up Jerusalem following the Babylonian exile, wields it like a weapon against Jews who had married "women—Ashdodites, Ammonites, Moabites" (Neh. 13:1–3, 23–27) and raised children who could not even speak Hebrew.

Against this background, we can see that our story begins with a scandal, a public scandal of major proportions. For "Ruth the Moabite," as she is repeatedly called by both the narrator and the characters in the story (1:22; 2:2, 21; 4:5, 10; cf. 2:6), is the great-grandmother of David. Her foreign bloodline runs through the royal house of Israel. One modern commentator suggests that it would be analogous to a grandchild of Hitler running for prime minister of the state of Israel (Neusner, *The Mother of the Messiah in Judaism*, 107). Yet as we shall see, this Moabite woman will reverse the expectations that attach to her nationality, or at least some of them. Like the "founding mother" of Moab, Lot's daughter, Ruth will be resourceful in preserving a family line in the face of extinction. Like the Moabite women of Peor (Num. 25), she will be sexually alluring to an Israelite man, and there will be important consequences. But in Ruth sexuality is linked with moral character of the highest kind. Therefore, it is no coincidence that through her sexual actions, not only is a family preserved, but the nation Israel is built up and (through the person of her great-grandson David) moved into deeper relationship with God.

Christian readers will note that the evangelist Matthew does not allow us to forget that Ruth is an ancestor of "Joseph the husband of Mary, of whom Jesus was born, who is called the Messiah" (Matt. 1:16). She is one of five women in Matthew's genealogy, the others being Tamar the Canaanite; Rahab, the harlot of Jericho; the (here unnamed) "wife of Uriah" (1:6); and Mary herself, pregnant and unwed. Each in her own way belongs to the shadow side of Israel's history and of ordinary human culture. All this, the evangelist implies, is part of the messy world that the Messiah comes to redeem.

Orpah . . . Ruth—Orpah's name, like those of Naomi's sons, bespeaks her destiny. However reluctantly, she will eventually turn her back on Naomi. Curiously, Ruth's name is not similarly transparent to meaning. One traditional rabbinic explanation is that it means "the one who fills to overflowing"; there is a possible philological connection to the verbal root *r-w-h*, "saturate." Moreover, such a connection makes thematic sense: Ruth does indeed fill Naomi's emptiness to overflowing. Nonetheless, the connection is far from obvious. And perhaps the very fact that Ruth's name cannot be fully "decoded" is itself one clue to the complexity of her character. Although she speaks only a few times, Ruth is the most fully developed character in the book; all the action revolves around her surprising initiatives. She cannot be reduced to a capsule description.

ten years—This seemingly perfunctory notice is the first of several instances in which the narrator invites inquiry by means of a gap or an ambiguity. The question here is, ten years from when? From their date of arrival, or from the time of these unpromising marriages, mentioned immediately before? The question is important, even if it is not finally resolvable. If it is the latter, then Ruth has been worn down by the long humiliation of barrenness before being widowed. This was the reading of the medieval rabbis, and that supposition greatly intensifies the effect of the narrator's single report of divine action: "And YHWH gave her pregnancy, and she bore a son" (4:13). Further, it gives credence to Ruth's strong attachment to her mother-in-law; at the time of widowhood, they have already lived together in the family compound for ten years. Christians might be interested in the rabbis' understanding, because it suggests that the messianic line of David *begins* with a miracle-touched birth.

On the other hand, maybe Naomi's boys were small when they went to Moab (as the woodcut portrays the scene), and they have been in Moab a total of "about ten years." So Ruth is a young widow, with her whole life ahead of her. This makes more remarkable her decision to leave all that is familiar; it would be so easy for her, being little more than a girl, to put this false start behind her and begin again in Moab. This interpretation may also explain Naomi's vehemence when she forbids the younger women to come: "It is very bitter for me because of you" (1:13). If the deaths of the sons have followed hard upon their foreign marriages, then it is likely that Naomi blames the young women for them. So there is the work not only of grief but also of reconciliation to be done as Naomi and Ruth walk toward Bethlehem.

Neither of these alternative interpretations is more inherently correct than the other. And while they are mutually exclusive as "historical" possibilities, maybe the storyteller deliberately leaves both open to our imaginations. For each of them leads us to see through the lens of the biblical text a somewhat different aspect of the human situation. Our reading is richer precisely because we can identify the sufferings and the achievements of these two women in more than one way.

5 *And the two of them also died, Maḥlon and Kilyon. And the woman was left without her two boys and without her husband.*

6 *And she arose, she and her bride-daughters, and she turned back from the fields of Moab. For she had heard in the field of Moab that YHWH had visited his people, to give them bread.*

1:5 *the woman was left without her two boys*—Although the two wives have been named, Naomi is at this point still "the woman" on whom the story focuses. The depth of her loss is registered in the reference to her dead sons as "her boys"; the Hebrew word is not normally applied to adults. But in fact, although Naomi's sons have married, they have remained immature from a genealogical standpoint. They have died, in effect, as children, leaving no children of their own to give them enduring memory. This is a profound personal tragedy, even deeper than we ourselves may feel, for the ancient Israelites had no consistent faith in the persistence of life on the other side of death.

1:6 *bride-daughters*—The basic meaning of the word *kallah* is "bride." When used in reference to a woman not newly married, it means "daughter-in-law." In the context of this story, the (otherwise ordinary) word acquires poignancy: these "brides" are in fact widows.

and she turned back—This verb (Heb. *shûv*) represents the central movement of the first part of the book; it occurs twelve times in the first chapter alone (vv. 6, 7, 8, 10, 11, 12, 15, 16, 21, 22). Repetition here underscores the thematic significance of the word, which elsewhere frequently represents a profound spiritual reorientation, a turning to God and away from sin or false worship (e.g., Deut. 4:30; Jer. 3:12, 14, 22). It is striking in this connection that Ruth is twice described as "the one who *turned back* with Naomi from the field of Moab" (1:22; 2:6). Although Ruth is not literally returning to Israel and its God, she and Naomi are equal partners in a radical reorientation.

she had heard in the field of Moab—The unusual emphasis on "the field" is noteworthy. In this book, the field rather than the city is the place where women's character is revealed. The public gate in the city is the meeting place of men, where legal arrangements are made (see 4:1–12). Yet it is significant that all the important initiatives involve the action of women "in the field." Up to this point, Naomi has been represented passively: she "was left" (vv. 3, 5). But now there begins a series of active verbs whose subject is Naomi and consequently her daughters-in-law: "she arose . . . she turned back . . . she went out . . . they walked." Although Naomi may be despairing (see v. 20), she nonetheless boldly undertakes the journey that will ultimately restore her joy.

YHWH—The abbreviation corresponds to the Hebrew letters that designate the "personal name" of God, revealed particularly to Israel (Exod. 3:15). The "ineffable Name" is considered by Jews too sacred to be pronounced aloud or even written in full. In English, the traditional substitute for this name is "the LORD."

And the woman was left without her two boys
and without her husband.
(Ruth 1:5)

7   *And she went out from the place where she had been, and her two bride-daughters with her. And they walked on the road, to turn back to the land of Judah.*

8   *And Naomi said to her two bride-daughters, "Go, turn back, each woman to the house of her mother. May YHWH do good-faith with you, just as you have done with the dead and with me.*

1:8 *the house of her mother*—This is one of only three instances in the Bible (cf. Song 3:4; 8:2) where the Israelite family unit is designated a "mother's house" instead of the usual "father's house." In all three places, the subject is romantic liaison. There is biblical evidence that occasionally, at least, the Israelite (or Moabite) mother played an important role in the arrangements for a child's marriage (see Gen. 24:67; 27:46; 28:2; Song 3:11). Further, in the context of this book, the unusual term quietly marks the fact that the book portrays the sphere of women and the power they wielded. This power would prove to be world shaping, even though in a traditional society such as Israel, the exercise of women's power was less publicly visible than that of men. A final inference might also be drawn from this phrase: Naomi is implicitly denying that she herself can function as mother to the young women. We shall see a gradual change in this position in the course of the book.

good-faith—The word is *ḥesed*, the essential quality of covenant relationship. Above all, *ḥesed* is the quality of generosity and loyalty demonstrated by Israel's God (e.g., Exod. 34:6). Secondarily, every person who enters into covenant with YHWH is expected to demonstrate that same quality. The prophet Micah offers the memorable instruction "And what does YHWH require of you—but to do justice, love *ḥesed*, and walk in humility with your God?" (Mic. 6:8). This, then, is no casual compliment that Naomi gives her Moabite "bride-daughters"; she tacitly includes them in the relationship that binds YHWH and Israel. Even more striking is the fact that she represents these foreign women as taking the initiative in doing *ḥesed*, providing a model that even YHWH would do well to emulate! We shall see that this distinctive quality of loyal kindness is the criterion on which human character is judged throughout the book.

9   *May YHWH grant it to you: Find rest, each woman in the house of her husband." And she kissed them. And they lifted up their voice and they wept.*

10   *And they said to her, "No, with you we will turn back to your people."*

11   *But Naomi said, "Turn back, my daughters. Why would you go with me? Do I still have sons in my belly, who might become husbands for you?*

1:9 *rest*—To Israelite ears, Naomi's instruction to "find rest" would not suggest that the younger women should find husbands to support them in a life of leisure. In the Bible, the word "rest" (Heb. *menuḥah*) does not connote relaxation in the conventional sense. Rather, it conveys a sense of deep belonging, of security. "Rest" is God's gift to Israel in bringing them into the promised land (Deut. 12:9; 1 Kgs. 8:56). "Rest" is the unshakable assurance that a person or a people feels in the presence of God, even when enemies threaten (Ps. 23:2; Isa. 32:18). Conversely, when Israel refuses to honor God, true rest is withheld from God's people (Ps. 95:11). Naomi is here indirectly invoking on her daughters-in-law the blessing of God's favor and continual presence, which gives freedom from the sources of deepest anxiety.

they lifted up their voice and they wept—This is familiar biblical idiom for weeping aloud. Nevertheless, the vivid picture it evokes should not be overlooked. This is full-voiced, full-bodied weeping. It is interesting, moreover, that in Hebrew idiom, "voice" is always a singular noun. It would not be incorrect to render it as "they lifted up their voices. . . ." However, I have left the singular form, because here the three women are fully joined in their grief. The woodcut that accompanies verse 1:14 shows them as a solid monolith of pain; the figures of the three women are barely distinguishable, one from another, in their common agony.

1:11 *my daughters*—The women are growing closer even as they dispute about what to do. Three times in as many verses, Naomi names them as her daughters, in contrast to the term "bride-daughters," which the narrator has used thus far. This remains her custom throughout the book.

sons in my belly—Under Israelite law, when a married man died childless, his brother was expected to marry the widow so she might remain within her adopted family (Deut. 25:5–10). Naomi here alludes to the established practice and at the same time shows how preposterous it would be to apply it in this case.

12   *Turn back, my daughters; go. For I am too old to have a husband. For if I said, 'I have hope . . .' Even if I had a husband tonight, and even birthed sons — would you then wait until they were grown?*

13   *Would you then hold back from having a husband? Don't, my daughters! For it is very bitter for me because of you. For the hand of YHWH has gone forth against me."*

1:13 *it is very bitter for me because of you*—Perhaps Naomi means that the tragedy of the young women's lives is her deepest source of pain, because she loves them. But it is possible that she means something quite different. She might also believe that these Moabite bride-daughters are the direct cause of her own tragic loss, that her sons' deaths were a punishment for marrying "infidels" (see the note at 1:4).

The Hebrew particle rendered "because" can also be a term of comparison, so an alternative translation is "it is much more bitter for me than for you." The younger women can begin again, with new families; Naomi's pleasure lies wholly in the past. There is no sense in their needlessly perpetuating the tragedy.

14   *And they lifted up their voice and wept still more. And Orpah kissed her mother-in-law. But Ruth stuck by her.*

15   *And she said, "Look, your sister-in-law has turned back to her people and to her gods. Turn back after your sister-in-law."*

1:14 *and Orpah kissed her*—Contemporary poet Thomas John Carlisle imagines Orpah departing from Naomi lovingly yet with a realistic awareness of the limits to her love. She knows "how easily a love aborts when driven to deeds beyond the feasible" (Carlisle, *Eve and After*, 58).

stuck by—The Hebrew verb *davaq* calls to mind what is perhaps the foremost biblical statement about the voluntary attachment of one person to another: "Therefore a man shall leave his father and his mother and stick by (traditionally, "cleave to") his wife, and they shall be one flesh" (Gen. 2:24). The echo may be deliberate. Although there is no indication of a sexual bond between the two women, Ruth is quietly making a bold statement of love in sticking by a woman whom others would see as God-forsaken. Thus she creates the foundation of love on which a new family structure will eventually be erected.

The word might also hint at something more than a personal bond. On several occasions *davaq* means adhering to God, either by Israel or by an individual: "After YHWH your God you shall walk, and him you shall fear, and his commandments you shall keep, and to his voice you shall listen, and him you shall serve, and by him you shall stick" (traditionally, "to him you shall hold fast"; Deut. 13:5 Heb. [4 Eng.]; see also Deut. 4:4; 10:20; Ps. 63:9 Heb. [8 Eng.]). Perhaps the narrator means for us to hear the Torah injunction echoing behind the forceful declaration of loyalty to Naomi *and her God* that Ruth will soon make. (On the ambiguity of this declaration, see below.)

1:15 *her gods*—For interpretation of this and the following verses, it is important to recognize that biblical Hebrew does not distinguish clearly between "god" (singular) and "gods" (plural). The word used here is *'elohîm*, the most general term for divinity; formally, it is a plural noun. When used for Israel's (emphatically) *one* God, the term is considered to be a "plural of majesty." (Compare Queen Victoria's legendary "We are not amused.") However, when used with reference to pagan worship, the same plural noun commonly denotes a multiplicity of deities. That is probably Naomi's intention here, although she might be thinking especially of Chemosh, the patron deity of the Moabites (Num. 21:29).

And they lifted up their voice and wept still more.
(Ruth 1:14)

16   *And Ruth said,*

      "Don't press me to leave you,

         to turn back from (following) after you.

         For where you go, I will go.

         And where you stay-the-night,

           I will stay.

         Your people (is) my people,

         and your God, my God.

1:16 *Don't press me to leave you*—This beautiful statement (it is in fact a small poem) is rightly one of the most beloved passages in the Bible. It is frequently read at weddings, and just because it is much used, we should be cautious of sentimentalizing it. This is a strong statement of devotion, yet the moment is not tender. Rather, the wills of these two determined women stand in acute tension at this point. That is probably why Ruth now speaks at length, for the first and only time in the book.

Your people (is) my people—I have departed from the standard translation, "Your people shall be my people," because the Hebrew clause does not include a verb in the future tense—or, in fact, a verb at all. A clause that is verbless in Hebrew normally is rendered in the present tense in English. One might argue (and the standard translation assumes) that the future tense is implied here by the surrounding clauses, which do include future-tense verbs. However, my more "wooden" translation suggests another possibility. All the other events mentioned here—going away, staying the night, dying—are projections into the future, which Ruth intends to share with Naomi. But Ruth may be saying that, as members of the same family, they *already* share two things—a people and a God. The translation I offer implies that what they already share is the basis for sharing all the contingencies in the near and far future.

and your God, my God—Because of this line, the poem is traditionally regarded as a classic confession of the convert's newfound faith in Israel's God. Indeed, female converts to Judaism frequently assume (for purposes of religious ceremony) the Hebrew name Ruth. The medieval rabbis upheld the primacy of Ruth's religious conviction: she has found the truth and is bound and determined to convert, even when Naomi lays out for her the rigorous demands of her new religion: no more visits to the theater or the circus (popular pagan diversions)!

Yet in fact, the narrative leaves open the question of how much Ruth knows about the religion she will practice in the land of Israel. Doubtless, she knows that Naomi worships a deity with a name different from those of her own ancestral gods. But is she fully aware that in crossing over the Jordan into Israel, she is committing herself to the exclusive worship of YHWH? In other words, when Ruth uses the word *'elohîm* here, does she mean God-with-a-capital-G, or does she think YHWH (whom she never specifically mentions throughout the book) is one among several gods whom she may worship in that place?

Ultimately, the question is whether the devotion Ruth declares here is primarily to Naomi's God or to Naomi herself. There are several reasons for thinking that the latter may be the case. First, the only specific religious reference—"and your God, my God"—is not prominent as either the first or the last line in the poem. Second, the closest analogue to this passage in the Bible is unquestionably the declaration of personal loyalty spoken by another foreigner to Ruth's great-grandson. When David is fleeing Jerusalem after Absalom's coup d'état, he tries to dissuade Ittai the Gittite from coming with him. Ittai has already been exiled once, David argues; why wander after the king into a precarious future? Thus David commands him, "I am going wherever I am going; go back . . . in loyalty and faithfulness!" But this time the Philistine soldier refuses to obey orders: "Wherever my lord the king is, whether for death or for life, there will your servant be!" (2 Sam. 15:20–21). His words echo Ruth's, and they get the same response: like Naomi, David acquiesces.

A third reason to think that Ruth is moved primarily by attachment to Naomi is simply that that is how many people come to God. The widely popular nineteenth-century Boston preacher Phillips Brooks, when asked what had led him to faith in Christ, answered, "I believe it was my Aunt Geneva." His answer may have disappointed the questioner, but in fact, it is sufficiently theological. Many, and perhaps most, people come to God because they know and love someone who knows and loves God.

But we cannot finally choose between the two interpretations, nor should we. They point to different ways that love of God and love of another human being may be bound together in our experience. Each kind of devotion may have temporal primacy and lead eventually to a deepening of the other.

And Ruth said, "Don't press me to leave you."
(Ruth 1:16)

17   *Where you die, I will die,*

           and there I will be buried.

           So may YHWH do to me,

           and may he add more to that —

           it is (only) death that will come

           between me and you."

18   *And she saw that she was determined to go with her,*

           and she gave up speaking to her.

1:17 *So may YHWH do*—In this typical oath formula, the divinely wrought penalty for violation is never named. Such oaths may have been in Israelite culture a fairly routine speech form, the equivalent of the English phrase "I swear." However, it is noteworthy that everywhere else in the Bible, the oath appears on the lips of a king or other leader of the people, and it has weighty public consequences (e.g., 1 Sam. 14:44; 2 Sam. 3:9; 1 Kgs. 2:23). It is possible, then, that when Ruth utters this oath, she unwittingly intimates her destiny as the ancestor of Israel's most important king.

it is (only) death—It is intriguing that Ruth's phrasing leaves the content of the oath ambiguous. It might also be translated: "if even death will come between me and you." Is Ruth bold enough to challenge even the finality of death?

1:18 *and she gave up speaking to her*—After Ruth's impassioned speech, Naomi lapses into silence. Is she moved beyond words? Perplexed by the young woman's tenacity? Or is she frustrated and frightened, feeling the burden of this young life, now inextricably bound to her own? The silent women, walking through the stark Judean wilderness on the way to Bethlehem, contrast sharply with those they will soon encounter: the "buzzing" female population of the town.

19   *And the two of them went on until they came to Bethle-hem. And it happened, when they came to Bethlehem, that the whole city was buzzing about them. And the women said, "Is this Naomi?"*

And the women said, "Is this Naomi?"
(Ruth 1:19)

20   *And she said to them,*

         "Don't call me Naomi ("My-pleasantness")!

         Call me Mara ("Bitterness"),

         for Shaddai has made it very bitter for me.

21   *I was full when I walked away,*

         but YHWH has brought me back empty.

         Why do you call me Naomi,

         when YHWH has testified against me,

         and Shaddai has done me evil?"

22   *And Naomi came back, and Ruth the Moabite, her bride-daughter, with her—the one who turned back from the fields of Moab. And they came to Bethlehem at the beginning of the barley harvest.*

1:20 *Shaddai*—Israel's earliest ancestors called their God by the name El Shaddai ("God Shaddai") before the name YHWH was revealed to Moses (Exod. 3:14–16; 6:3). Although this ancient name is often rendered in English translations as "God Almighty," the Hebrew does not support that interpretation, and it is better to leave "Shaddai" untranslated. More important than translation are the associations of the name. In almost every instance of its appearance in the ancestral stories, it is associated with God's promise that the ancestors—the founders of the Israelite people—will have offspring in abundance (Gen. 17:1–2; 28:3; 35:11; 48:3–4; 49:25). Surely the audience is meant to detect an echo of that promise and blessing here.

But a second association is also apt and may better reflect Naomi's present state of mind. Apart from Genesis, Job is the book where God is most often named as Shaddai. There it denotes a God whose immense and sometimes hostile power is to be feared by those who know what God can do. Naomi's next words are, like Job's, a poetic cry of rage and pain.

A third association might also be mentioned. The name Shaddai seems to derive from an ancient Semitic word meaning "mountain" (*shadû* in the old Babylonian language); probably, the name originally denoted a mountain deity. But in Hebrew, the same word might be understood as meaning "my breasts." (The two meanings of *shaddai* are perhaps homonyms, with no intrinsic connection between them. On the other hand, there may be something more than sheer coincidence at work. After all, mountains and breasts have the same approximate shape, and so in its early history the word might have designated something mound-shaped.) This coincidence of meanings for Shaddai may be significant in the context of our story. For Naomi presents herself as a woman whose body has been emptied of all possibility of nurturance. Could this bitter naming of God as Shaddai be a reminder of her own breasts, which once nurtured sons who are no more? At the end of the book, she will in fact hold another son to her body, and that expresses Naomi's own restoration to full life.

has made it very bitter for me—Twice more (see 1:13) Naomi reiterates the bitterness that contradicts her name. This could also be translated "Shaddai has greatly embittered me." If indeed the bitterness has entered into her character, then that might explain both Naomi's silence toward Ruth and her fourfold accusation against God in this verse and the next.

1:21 *testified against me*—Naomi's own poetic outburst is clearly a religious statement, and an outraged one. She represents Shaddai as her adversary in a legal suit. The term normally refers to human testimony (e.g., Num. 35:30), and sometimes to false witness (Deut. 19:16). No one else in the Bible uses the term to characterize God's "prosecution." At this moment the two women stand in counterpoint. Ruth has just laid claim, through Naomi, to the God whom her mother-in-law accuses of having "done [her] evil."

It is striking that Naomi does not comment on Ruth's arrival with her in Bethlehem. Is Naomi's pain and alienation from God so deep that she cannot even acknowledge the potential comfort of human companionship? Or perhaps she is trying to protect her daughter-in-law from attention that could easily turn hostile. At the point of entry into Bethlehem, the narrator mentions three times that Ruth is from Moab (1:22; 2:2); thus we are reminded how these small-town Israelites must see her (see also 2:6).

1:22 *at the beginning of the barley harvest*—The barley harvest marks the beginning of the grain-harvest season (April to June), when migrant workers would be most likely to find both work and food in plenty within an agricultural community such as Bethlehem.

After the steady downward spiral of the first chapter, culminating in Naomi's outburst, the narrator's simple prose statement summarizes and concludes the first movement of the story.

CHAPTER TWO

Gleaning

1   *(Naomi has a kinsman of her husband, a man of considerable substance, from Elimelekh's ancestral family, and his name is Boaz.)*

2:1 *Naomi has a kinsman*—The grammatical form of the narrator's aside, addressed to the reader, stands out slightly from the rest of the story. While the other sentences have verbs in the past tense, here there are two clauses, verbless in Hebrew, that are best rendered in the English present tense. The effect is to suggest direct interaction between the narrator and the reader.

a man of considerable substance—The phrase is ambiguous in Hebrew, as in English. It could be rendered, somewhat more literally, as "a man mighty-in-strength" or "a mighty man of valor." The phrase may connote physical power; most often, it is used in reference to warriors. But Boaz is no longer a young man, and so here other connotations seem more likely. First, in this context the term connotes the power conferred by material prosperity; Boaz is a relatively wealthy man in his small community. Further, the term suggests something about Boaz's moral character. He is a man of considerable substance (*ḥayîl*, Exod. 18:21, 25) in that sense as well. Both these connotations will be developed as the story proceeds.

ancestral family—The ancestral family was the intermediate unit of social organization between the tribe and the multigenerational household, normally called the "father's house." Although lacking the extensive social and economic powers associated with a true clan system, this cluster of households related by blood and marriage provided some degree of social cohesion, offering protection to its weaker members and laying obligation upon the stronger ones.

Boaz—The name does not appear elsewhere as a personal name, but it is attached (somewhat strangely) to one of the two great freestanding pillars outside Solomon's temple (1 Kgs. 7:21). The Hebrew word means "in him is strength"; probably, the pillar is thus named in order to invoke God's might on behalf of the temple, the city, and her people. While the Bible never draws a connection between the man named Boaz and the famous pillar, one might see in his name an intimation, first, of his own strength of character, but more, of God's protective power operative through him (see the notes at 3:9).

And his name is Boaz.
(Ruth 2:1)

2   *And Ruth the Moabite said to Naomi, "So, I'm going to go to the field and glean among the ears, behind someone in whose eyes I find favor." And she said to her, "Go ahead, my daughter."*

3   *And she went and came to the field and gleaned behind the harvesters. And by chance she happened upon the portion of the field belonging to Boaz, the one from Elimelekh's ancestral family.*

4   *And along came Boaz from Bethlehem! And he said to the harvesters, "YHWH be with you!" And they said to him, "May YHWH bless you!"*

2:2 *So, I'm going to go . . . and glean*—The Hebrew phrasing suggests that Ruth's tone is one of resolve. Determination seems to be characteristic of her (see 1:18)—in this case, determination both to get food and to spare Naomi, whose strength and spirits have been exhausted by the journey.

and glean—The Hebrew verb *laqaṭ* occurs twelve times in the chapter (vv. 2, 3, 7, 8, 15, 16, 17, 18, 19, 23), always with Ruth as its grammatical subject. The unusual repetition serves to highlight the fact that Ruth is not an ordinary hired worker. Rather, she comes under the protection of the Israelite practice—in fact, it was a law, an indispensable element of Israel's practical religion—of deliberately leaving some grain in the field. The unharvested grain was to be gleaned by the most vulnerable members of society: widows, orphans, and sojourners (Deut. 24:19–22; cf. Lev. 19:9–10; 23:22). These categories accurately describe the current status of Ruth and Naomi.

behind someone in whose eyes I find favor—The unusual and somewhat awkward phrase may also indicate that, for all her determination, Ruth feels her vulnerability and potential for attracting negative attention as a "Moabite."

2:3 *And by chance she happened upon*—While the narrative speaks in terms of happenstance rather than providence, here it lays special emphasis upon a "chance occurrence" that will prove to be a source of blessing. Naomi's outcry against God (1:20–21) has already alerted us to consider how God's action—for good or for ill—may be a hidden factor in this story.

2:4 *YHWH be with you! . . . May YHWH bless you!*—These may have been conventional greetings (cf. Ps. 129:8), but the fact that the narrator takes the trouble to record them emphasizes that the relations between Boaz and his workers are cordial. Perhaps the narrator means to imply even more—namely, that Boaz's relationships are ultimately governed by a lively awareness of God as the Source of blessing and the One to whom we must answer for our treatment of others.

5   *And Boaz said to his worker-lad, the one who supervised the harvesters, "To whom does this worker-girl belong?"*

6   *And the worker-lad who supervised the harvesters answered and said, "She is a Moabite worker-girl, who turned back with Naomi from the field of Moab.*

7   *And she said, 'Please let me glean, and I will gather among the cut ears behind the harvesters.' And she came and stood from morning up till now. There has been little of this sitting in the 'house' for her!"*

8   *And Boaz said to Ruth, "Haven't you heard, my daughter? Don't go gleaning in another field. No, you shouldn't go anywhere else. You should stick with my worker-girls here.*

2:5 *worker-lad . . . worker-girl*—The terms are masculine and feminine forms of the same word: *na'ar* and *na'arah*. Here they denote both youth (relative to Boaz) and social status. It is possible that the terms apply specifically to those who have lost their family land and therefore work for others, either as permanent debt slaves or as seasonal agricultural workers. The feminine form can also designate a woman of marriageable age.

To whom . . . ?—Boaz's question concerning the stranger who has appeared among his regular workers might mean one of several things. One possibility is "For whom is she working?"—the implication being "I didn't hire her!" Or perhaps this Moabite differs somewhat in dress and manner from the Israelite women. So the question might mean "To what people does she belong?" As a chief man in the village, Boaz has a concern, maybe even a responsibility, to assign this stranger to a certain social niche. So a third possibility is that he is inquiring about her family connections (maybe he imagines that she is a resident of another village who has for some reason lost her immediate family and been forced to come to distant relatives in Bethlehem). Finally (and not excluding any of the preceding suggestions), Boaz, as a man without a wife, may have a personal interest in this (evidently) attractive young woman. So he might be wondering, "Is she 'available'?"

2:7 *There has been little of this sitting in the "house" for her!*—It seems that the two men are observing Ruth as she takes a short break in a thatch-covered shelter (the "house") set up in the field to give the workers shade.

2:8 *Haven't you heard . . . ?*—Boaz's approach to Ruth is abrupt. He sounds as if he is more accustomed to giving orders than to courting. The next verse indicates what he might expect Ruth to have heard: he has already given his workers orders about how they are to treat her.

You should stick with—The verb is the same one (Heb. *davaq*) used in 1:14. Repetitions of the relatively rare verb (see also 2:21, 23) emphasize and make memorable Ruth's original action of "sticking by" Naomi. Moreover, they hint at the fact that Ruth's own exceptional loyalty to Naomi is beginning to find an echo in Boaz's protective regard for this courageous yet still vulnerable foreign woman.

And Boaz said to his worker-lad . . . ,
"To whom does this worker-girl belong?"
(Ruth 2:5)

9   *(Keep) your eyes on the field where they are harvesting and walk behind the women. Haven't I ordered the worker-lads not to touch you? When you get thirsty, go to the jars and drink from what the worker-lads draw."*

10   *And she fell on her face and bowed to the ground. And she said to him, "Why have I found favor in your eyes, that you would give me recognition—and I am nothing but a foreigner!?"*

11   *And Boaz answered and said to her, "Of course it has been told to me—everything that you have done for your mother-in-law after the death of your husband, that you left-behind your father and your mother and the land where you were born and went to a people you didn't know at all a day or two ago!*

2:10 *And she fell on her face and bowed to the ground.*—Ruth's gesture is exceptional; it is far beyond the ordinary response of a servant to a master. Therefore, it is important to consider whether it is subservience that Ruth is expressing (as one might first suppose) or perhaps something else. Prostration in Israelite culture was an expression of profound respect. Most often, we see biblical characters bowing before God or before one whom God has anointed: the king or a prophet. But it was not necessarily a gesture of subordination. One might compare Ruth's act here to that of Abigail when she meets David for the first time (1 Sam. 25:23). This is another case of a woman bowing before the man whom she will one day marry. Yet if Abigail comes to David as a petitioner, she comes also as an adviser, to keep him from getting entangled unnecessarily in a blood feud. This David recognizes, and he blesses both God and Abigail for her good sense. In light of the larger story of David, one might say that Abigail is not prostrating herself before the hotheaded young outlaw that David is on the day she meets him. Rather, the alert reader can see that she is offering the appropriate response to YHWH's anointed—whether or not she consciously recognizes him as such. Similarly, Ruth's gesture expresses her deep gratitude for Boaz's unexpected generosity, but it may also be an early signal to the reader that a larger plan of God is somehow at work through this man. Recognition of the hidden action of God will deepen and be confirmed as the story proceeds.

2:11 *you left-behind your father and your mother and the land where you were born*—Boaz vividly describes Ruth's heroic act of leaving behind not only all that was familiar but, more than that, the only security and protection the young widow might have expected to have. Probably, we are meant to recall Abraham, whose call from God came in almost identical language: "Get you going, from your land and from the place where you were born" (Gen. 12:1). Ancient peoples generally regarded leaving one's birthplace as a trauma and calamity, not an opportunity. Ruth's situation might be seen as even more precarious than Abraham's, for she took this step without a specific call and promise from God.

12   *May YHWH repay your action, and may your recom-*
     pense be complete from YHWH the God of Israel,
     under whose wings you have come to take shelter."

13   *And she said, "May I continue to find favor in your*
     eyes, my lord! Indeed, you have comforted me and spo-
     ken to the heart of your servant-girl—and I am not
     (even) like one of your own servant-girls!"

2:12 *YHWH the God of Israel, under whose wings*—This may be the most purely "religious" statement thus far in the book. Boaz commends Ruth to the care of the God she has newly embraced, using traditional language drawn indirectly from Israel's prayers, the Psalms:

> With his wingspan he will hide you,
> and under his wings you will take shelter.
>
> (Ps. 91:4)

> How precious is your goodness (*ḥesed*), O God!
> And human beings—in the shadow of your wings they take shelter.
>
> (Ps. 36:8 Heb. [7 Eng.])

In fact, Boaz's prayer will begin to be realized in a way he does not foresee, when Ruth takes the bold initiative of seeking shelter under his "wing" (see 3:9)!

2:13 *spoken to the heart*—The phrase means to speak reassuringly, bringing real comfort (cf. Gen. 50:21; Isa. 40:2), but it can also denote romantic speech (Gen. 34:3; Judg. 19:3; Hos. 2:16 Heb. [14 Eng.]). Ruth's words are deferential, but already it is clear that she does not intend to let Boaz get away with pious platitudes. She wants tangible signs of "favor" from Boaz himself!

and I am not (even) like one of your own servant-girls!—The statement is ambiguous. At first hearing, it seems to mean that Ruth is less deserving of Boaz's favor than are those who regularly work for him. (The servant-girl was at the lowest level of inclusion within the protective circle of the Israelite "father's house.") But maybe Ruth is also beginning to differentiate herself positively from the other servants and is hoping that Boaz will notice the difference. The next verse indicates that he does.

*"Indeed, you have comforted me and spoken
to the heart of your servant-girl."*
(Ruth 2:13)

14   *And Boaz said to her at mealtime, "Come here and eat some of the bread, and dip your piece in the sour-wine." And she sat to one side of the harvesters, and he poured out for her roasted grain, and she ate and was satisfied and had-some-left-over.*

2:14 *sour-wine*—For the poor, sour-wine was the alternative to olive oil for moistening and flavoring bread.

he poured out for her—Boaz goes far beyond the water he initially offered (v. 9). Not only does he give her a substantial meal, but he serves her himself. In the ancient world, for a man to serve food to a woman was a highly unusual gesture—to say nothing of the difference in social status between Ruth and Boaz.

had-some-left-over—The phrase is a single word in Hebrew, but it says a great deal about both Boaz and Ruth. First, it speaks to Boaz's generosity: he gives Ruth more than enough to satisfy her. Yet even more, it speaks of the consideration that Ruth shows for her mother-in-law. She is ever mindful of Naomi, even on an occasion when she might be excused for relaxing and forgetting, at least for a little while.

And Boaz said to her at mealtime, "Come here and eat some of the bread, and dip your piece in the sour-wine."
(Ruth 2:14)

15   *And she got up to glean. And Boaz commanded his worker-lads: "She may glean also among the cut ears—and don't you harass her!*

16   *And also, you should go ahead and pull some out of the bundles for her, and leave-(it)-behind, and she will glean—and don't you give her a hard time!"*

17   *And she gleaned in the field until the evening. And she threshed what she had gleaned, and it was about an ephah of barley!*

2:15 *She may glean also among the cut ears*—We already know that Ruth is a hard worker (2:7), and now she is granted extraordinary privileges. Ordinary "charity" to the poor would confine gleaners to the unharvested edges of the field, or they might pick up the few cut ears inadvertently left behind by the hired hands. (Israelite law specifically forbade landowners from going back over their fields to collect the cut ears that had been forgotten; see Deut. 24:19.) But Boaz seeks to make her work easier and maximize her intake, even instructing his workers to pull some ears out of the bundles they have already gathered.

2:17 *an ephah*—Because of the special favor Ruth enjoys, she collects enough grain by the end of the day to sustain her and Naomi for some weeks. An ephah is a large dry measure. Its size is uncertain; estimates range from twenty-two to thirty-nine liters. This quantity of barley would then weigh at least thirty pounds, and possibly as much as fifty. This is a (literally) staggering amount for a worker to take home. (Ancient Babylonian texts indicate that rations for male workers were one or two pounds per day.) The surprising turn of events will jolt Naomi into a radically different frame of mind.

18   *And she lifted it and came to the city, and her mother-*
      in-law saw what she had gleaned. And she brought out
      and gave her what she had-left-over after she was
      satisfied.

19   *And her mother-in-law said to her, "Where did you*
      glean today? And wherever have you been working?
      May the one who gives you recognition be blessed!"
      And she told her mother-in-law with whom she had
      been working. She said, "The name of the man with
      whom I was working today is Boaz."

20   *And Naomi said to her bride-daughter, "May he be*
      blessed by YHWH, the one who has not abandoned his
      good-faith with the living and with the dead!" And
      Naomi said to her, "The man is kin to us; he is one of
      our redeemers."

2:18 *after she was satisfied*—The repeated comment (cf. v. 14) underscores the fact that Ruth's new condition of being full contrasts completely with Naomi's portrayal of herself as having returned utterly "empty" (1:21). Naomi has been almost wordless since her return. But now words begin to pour out of her.

2:19 *May the one who gives you recognition be blessed!*—Naomi, who has felt herself accursed, now erupts in blessing. Unwittingly, in blessing a man whose name she does not yet know, she echoes the blessing that Boaz's own workers gave to him (2:4). The events of the next two chapters show the realization of that blessing.

"Recognition" may seem a slight favor for Boaz to grant—until we recall that Ruth is a stranger, a foreigner. Ancient Israel was a kinship-based society, in which ancestral ties to a particular location constituted the most important element of one's personal identity. Lacking such a connection to Bethlehem, Ruth the Moabite is in a sense unrecognizable. In the next chapter, we shall see her coming fully into her own identity—significantly, in Boaz's presence, on the threshing floor.

2:20 *abandoned (left-behind)*—This verb (Heb. *'azav*) is repeated several times throughout the chapter, and this allows the reader or hearer to perceive a connection among a series of exceptional events that, it turns out, disclose the moral qualities of Ruth and Boaz. Boaz knows of Ruth as the woman who was bold and loyal enough to "leave-behind" (or "abandon") father and mother and birthplace (2:11) and become wholly vulnerable, not only a voluntary exile but one with an old woman to support. (We readers also recall her strong injunction to Naomi, "Don't press me to leave you," 1:16.) Moreover, Boaz responds to her act of generous "abandon" with a corresponding action of "leaving-behind" grain (v. 16). Now Naomi blesses Boaz as a man who has not abandoned good-faith (*ḥesed;* see the note at 1:8) with the living or the dead. The ambiguity of the previous blessing seems even stronger here. The blessing falls first on Boaz, but the scope of this kindness (to "the living [or] the dead") seems to go beyond what Boaz himself has done and to encompass God's *ḥesed*, which reaches back even beyond the grave.

The man is kin to us—It is noteworthy that at the same time Naomi claims kinship with Boaz, she also claims Ruth more fully. Once she told Ruth to go back to her own family (1:8); now Boaz is "kin to *us*."

one of our redeemers—Naomi refers to the Israelite practice of land redemption: when a debt-encumbered farmer had to sell the ancestral plot of land, a more prosperous member of the extended family circle was obligated to buy it back (Lev. 25:23–28, 47–49). The goal of the law was for Israel to remain from generation to generation a nation of free peasants working their own land and not to devolve into a feudal system of rich landowners and serfs.

And her mother-in-law saw what she had gleaned.
(Ruth 2:18)

21 *And Ruth the Moabite said, "He even said to me, 'You should stick with the workers who work for me until they finish all the harvesting for me.'"*

22 *And Naomi said to Ruth her bride-daughter, "It's good, my daughter, that you go out with his worker-girls, and they won't press themselves on you in another field."*

23 *And she stuck by Boaz's worker-girls for gleaning until completion of the barley harvest and the wheat harvest. And she settled in with her mother-in-law.*

2:22 *you go out with his worker*-girls—Ruth is not quite right in her report of Boaz's instructions, and Naomi offers this subtle and protective correction. Ruth remembers that she is supposed to stick with Boaz's "workers" (the term here is in masculine gender, often used with reference to a mixed group of both women and men). But in fact, Boaz specified that Ruth should stick with the *women* (2:8). Maybe it is due to her youth that Ruth is inattentive to propriety (and possible danger). But there may also be a cultural difference. It is likely that Ruth's original family were pastoral nomads "in the fields of Moab" (1:1, 6; 2:6), an area where seasonal nomads have followed traditional routes to pasturage for thousands of years. She may have experienced more informal mingling of men and women in shared work in the fields and therefore be unaware of the stricter separation between the sexes that obtains in the more sedentary, "urban" environment of Bethlehem.

press themselves on you—This is the same word Ruth uses when she tells Naomi, "Don't press me" (1:16). The word implies a certain amount of pressure, emotional and even physical; here it seems to be specifically sexual pressure that Naomi wishes her "daughter" to avoid. Boaz has already instructed his workers not to touch Ruth (2:9); clearly, a strange woman in the fields is likely to be subject to such pressure.

2:23 *the barley harvest and the wheat harvest*—The two harvests occur in succession. The comment indicates that a fairly long time has elapsed, perhaps three months, before the next scene takes place.

CHAPTER THREE

Who Are You, My Daughter?

1   And Naomi, her mother-in-law, said to her, "My daughter, shall I not seek for you a resting-place, one that will be good for you?

2   And now, isn't Boaz our kinsman? — the one with whose worker-girls you have been. And look, he is winnowing (at) the barley threshing floor tonight.

3:1 *a resting-place*—What Naomi desires for the younger woman has not changed (see 1:9). What has changed is that the woman who once felt old and bitter now believes herself capable of helping provide what she desires for her "daughter." Previously, we have seen Ruth's commitment to "stick by" Naomi. Now, for the first time, we see Naomi making the reciprocal commitment to seek Ruth's welfare. With a rapid series of leading questions and direct orders, she enlists the younger woman in her plan.

3   *Now wash up, and anoint yourself, and put on your best dress, and go down to the threshing floor. Do not make yourself known to the man until he has finished eating and drinking.*

4   *And then, when he lies down, and you know the spot where he is lying, you go and uncover the place-of-his-feet and lie down. And he will tell you what you should do."*

3:3 *go down to the threshing floor*—In an ancient settlement, the public threshing floor was located in a place where the wind was strong enough to blow away the chaff from the tossed grain. In nearby Jerusalem, "the threshing floor of Aravnah the Jebusite" (2 Sam. 24:16) was a small rock plateau at a high point just outside the city wall; three generations hence, King David would acquire it as the building site for God's house. In Bethlehem, the fields and the threshing floor lay in the valley below the city.

As the verse suggests, the threshing floor was known as a place for hard drinking; the work of threshing and winnowing was hot, and breathing the chaff was parching. The threshing floor was also, it seems, one of the few places in a small town or village where there was opportunity for sexual laxity. The prophet Hosea, denouncing Israel's unfaithfulness to God, assumes that everyone will understand his metaphor of the prostitute on the threshing floor:

> You have whored away from your God;
>   you have loved a whore's-hire on all the grain floors.
>   (Hos. 9:1)

In her own way, Naomi plots to use the threshing floor to her (and Ruth's) advantage.

3:4 *uncover the place-of-his-feet and lie down*—Naomi's phrasing is deliberately indirect, since "feet" (or "legs") is sometimes in Hebrew a circumlocution for the male genitals. Nonetheless, there is no mistaking the fact that she is asking Ruth to take an initiative no less daring and dangerous than Ruth's own decision to come to Judah. That this initiative is a sexual one is underscored by repetition of the verb "lie down" (*shakhav*), which occurs eight times in the chapter (vv. 4, 7, 8, 13, 14). In biblical Hebrew, the verb often implies sexual activity (as does the phrase "sleep with" in contemporary English).

Some commentators consider that Naomi is exploiting the attractive young woman for her own benefit. Certainly, some measure of economic desperation motivates Naomi's plan. The harvest is over (2:23), and with it ends the steady food supply for gleaners. It promises to be a lean winter for two women who are leading a literally hand-to-mouth existence. Moreover, Ruth will no longer be daily in Boaz's sight; Naomi may well fear that she will also be out of his mind and he will forget all about his poor relations. So she has good reason to be anxious. But does she act selfishly in propelling Ruth into this highly vulnerable situation on the threshing floor? In fact, Ruth is the only one of the two women who can take the necessary risk, for she is the one who is still marriageable, in Israelite terms. (The primary aim of Israelite marriage was children; that one might marry for companionship in old age is a modern notion.) On her side, Naomi has had three months to observe Boaz and learn the public reputation of this "man of considerable substance" (2:1). Has she calculated the risk with sufficient care? Has she accurately assessed his character and his regard for Ruth? These questions must be in Naomi's mind as Ruth goes down to the threshing floor.

And he *will tell you*—Naomi is experienced in the ways of men in a traditional society; after all, she has been married and has reared two sons. So Naomi knows that in this situation the personal initiative must seem to rest with Boaz and that the outcome will surely depend upon his public action. Yet if Boaz does indeed care for Ruth, then why has he let the three months of harvest time elapse without expressing his feelings or intentions toward her? Perhaps this dignified older man is nervous about offering himself to a young woman (see 3:10). Perhaps the respected Israelite elder still has to overcome his own prejudice against taking a Moabite wife.

With this element of uncertainty looming large, what is most striking in the scene that now unfolds is the profound mutual trust expressed by Naomi, Ruth, and Boaz. Each of them ultimately stakes everything on the good judgment and good-faith (*ḥesed*) of the others. Only through the genuine caring of each of the three can urgent need—and now, the possibility of deep humiliation—turn into something completely different, namely, fulfillment and rest.

"Now wash up, and anoint yourself, and put on your best dress,
and go down to the threshing floor."
(Ruth 3:3)

5   *And she said to her, "Everything that you say, I will do."*

6   *And she went down to the threshing floor, and she did everything as her mother-in-law had commanded her.*

3:5 *Everything that you say, I will do.*—In this and the following verse, the narrative places unusual emphasis on Ruth's precise execution of Naomi's command. Moreover, the strong word "command" is unexpected in this context. Elsewhere in the Bible, it is almost always God who is said to "command." So the reader's attention may be arrested here long enough to notice that the phrasing in these two verses does in fact have a familiar ring: this is the language used when the right response is given to commands that come from God. In fact, such an obedient response is a relatively rare occurrence in the Bible. Therefore, it is easy to link the phrasing here with the few instances in which we do see ready compliance with God's commands. Ruth's reply is a near quote of Israel's initial eager response to God at Sinai: "Everything that YHWH has spoken, we will do!" (Exod. 19:8). In that case, the desire for obedience proved to be short-lived (see Exod. 32). But the situation here is different, as the next verse shows.

3:6 *and she did everything as her mother-in-law had commanded her*—Ruth's action is as good as her word; she perfectly executes the "command" she has been given. The language of the verse is again a near quote of the foundational narrative of Torah, which on two occasions reports only that someone "did everything as God had commanded": when Noah built the ark (Gen. 6:22; 7:5) and again when Israel built the desert tabernacle (Exod. 39:32, 43).

The technique of quoting the tradition in this verse and the preceding one has implications for our understanding of the present story. First, the very similarity of wording underscores the contrast between the conduct of Ruth, the obedient foreigner, and that of Israel. Further, it may suggest that behind Naomi's peremptory "commands" is another level of authority, namely, God's own.

7   *And Boaz ate and drank, and his heart was good. And he went to lie down at the edge of the heap. And she went softly and uncovered the place-of-his-feet, and she lay down.*

8   *And it happened, at midnight, that the man trembled and twisted around—and here is a woman lying at the place-of-his-feet!*

3:7 *softly*—The word appears only a few times in the Bible, and always it denotes action that is accomplished with skill and subtlety. Elsewhere it is used of beguiling speech (1 Sam. 18:22), of stealthy action (1 Sam. 24:4), and even of the magic arts practiced in Pharaoh's court (Exod. 7:22; 8:3, 14 Heb. [8:7, 18 Eng.]).

3:8 *trembled*—At first glance, the word (Heb. *ḥarad*) does not seem to require comment. There is nothing unusual about a man sleeping in an exposed area shivering from the night chill. Yet this is one of several times in this scene when a word or phrase is chosen that appears elsewhere in the Bible with reference to God's presence and authority (see the notes at 3:5 and 3:6). Most memorably, when God descended upon Sinai in thunder, fire, and smoke, both the people and the mountain "trembled" (Exod. 19:16, 18). Again, in the book of Job, Elihu's heart "trembles" at God's voice (37:1). Similarly, the verb denotes the deference, or fear, associated with God's anointed, the king (1 Sam. 13:7; 1 Kgs. 1:49). Ancient Near Eastern kings were not wholly secular figures; the awe, or fear, that attached to the king derived from his divine anointing (see Ps. 2:6–7), as well as from his political power. So while the word *ḥarad* makes good literal sense in this context, it seems also to hint that God's authority and presence are discernible beneath the surface of the narrative.

and here is a woman—The Hebrew text here uses a participial clause, which creates a sense of immediacy for the reader. We are with Boaz, looking through his eyes, in this moment of surprised discovery.

9   *And he said, "Who are you?" And she said, "I am Ruth, your maidservant. Now spread your 'wing' over your maidservant, for you are a redeemer."*

10   *And he said, "Blessed are you to YHWH, my daughter! You have made your last act-of-good-faith better than the first, in not going after the men-in-their-prime, whether poor or rich.*

3:9 *Who are you?*—Boaz's question is the obvious one for him to ask under the circumstances, but there is more to the question than is immediately obvious. This is the second of three times that the question of Ruth's identity is posed in the course of the story. The first time Boaz saw the young foreigner in the field, he asked, *"To whom* does this worker-girl belong?" (2:5). At that time she had no independent identity in his eyes: she must "belong" to someone—a family, an employer. But that has now changed, as is evident from the form of his question. Here on the threshing floor, he asks Ruth to name her own identity. Her reply is remarkable in that she does not stop at naming herself; she goes on to confront Boaz with a thus-far neglected element of his own identity, namely, that of redeemer.

I am Ruth, your maidservant—This is the first time Ruth's name is spoken by any character in the story (contrast 2:6, where she is initially described to Boaz as "a Moabite worker-girl," and 2:8, where he calls her "my daughter"). She speaks here in a manner that is both forthright and modest, identifying herself first by name and only afterward as Boaz's subordinate. Moreover, Ruth makes a subtle but important change in the way she characterizes her relationship to Boaz. Earlier she called herself a "servant-girl" (see the note at 2:13); now she uses a term for a household member of more elevated standing. Although both words are deferential, the shift between the two may mean that she is now consciously representing herself as a prospect for marriage to this man.

spread your "wing"—Regardless of their difference in social status, Ruth does not hesitate to give Boaz instruction. In this context, the "wing" is the fold of Boaz's clothing. Elsewhere in the Bible, the image of a man "spreading his wing" over a woman connotes the social and economic protection of marriage (Ezek. 16:8), and that is clearly what Ruth is asking for. But in this literary context, the metaphor acquires additional meaning. Boaz earlier used the metaphor of wings when he commended Ruth to God's protection (2:12). Now, in asking that he spread his own wing over her, she says, in effect, "You act on God's behalf to make your prayer a reality!" As the next note suggests, the words that follow strengthen that implicit demand.

It is often debated whether in fact sexual intercourse took place between Ruth and Boaz on the threshing floor. Although strong opinions are expressed on both sides, the text itself is silent and therefore ambiguous. We must conclude that from the perspective of the narrator, settling the matter beyond reasonable doubt is simply not the point.

you are a redeemer—Ruth has in mind something beyond the ordinary meaning of this term in the context of the legal institution of land redemption (see the note at 2:20). Although the financial situation of the two women is precarious, evidently Naomi still holds some family land (see 4:5). So when Ruth names Boaz as "redeemer," she is doing something more than claiming the minimal security that Israelite law guaranteed to the poor. We have already seen that she is asking for marriage. Yet the word "redeemer" is not just a circumlocution for that. Rather, it follows in the literary pattern we have already noted in this threshing-floor scene. In the overwhelming majority of its occurrences in the Bible, the one so named is God. Therefore, this is another word that points to the operation of God's character and intention through human agency.

"Redeemer" is the way God is named in Israel by those whose situation is desperate, those for whom all human help is insufficient. He is the strong Redeemer of orphans, whose fields the powerful would usurp (Prov. 23:10–11). The psalmist praises God the Redeemer, who saves his "life from the pit" (Ps. 103:4). Perhaps the oldest hymn recorded by Israel praises God for "redeeming" the people from slavery in Egypt (Exod. 15:13). And many centuries later, when Israel experiences its greatest historical and theological trauma—the destruction of Jerusalem and its temple and the exile of its inhabitants to Babylon—there arises a great prophet who over and over names God as the one who is still powerful to act as Israel's Redeemer. The anonymous prophet known as Second Isaiah offers this unforgettable assurance to a defeated and prostrate people:

> Yes, I YHWH your God am holding you by the hand.
> I am the one who says to you, "Do not be afraid."
>   I myself am helping you.
> Do not be afraid, you worm Jacob,
>   people of Israel.
> I myself am helping you (an utterance of YHWH).
>   And (I am) your Redeemer, the Holy One of Israel.
>   (Isa. 41:13–14; see also 43:1, 14; 44:6, 22–24; etc.)

When Boaz the "redeemer" tells Ruth, "Do not be afraid" (3:11), are we then meant to hear an echo of God's assurance to the desperate?

3:10 *act-of-good-faith*—The phrase renders the Hebrew word *ḥesed* (see the note at 1:8).

And he said, "Who are you?"
(Ruth 3:9)

11   *And now, my daughter, do not be afraid. Everything that you say, I will do for you. For all the gate-assembly of my people knows that you are a valorous woman.*

3:11 *all the gate-assembly of my people*—The Hebrew literally reads "the whole gate of my people." The phrase, which occurs only here, vividly evokes a picture of life in an Israelite town or village, where the chief place of public gathering was the public square inside the gate. It was a gathering place primarily for men, namely, the "elders," the adult male householders, who gathered to make decisions affecting the well-being of the community. But women had an indirect presence at the town gate. While they did not generally hold public office (Deborah being an exception; see Judg. 4:4–9; 5:7), women were primary economic producers, teachers, preservers, and propagators of culture in ancient Israel. The home was the chief place of learning (formal schooling was a rarity) and also of economic production in a subsistence-level, agrarian society. Women worked mostly at home and perhaps rarely spoke in public on community matters. Yet their character and their work were no less essential to the well-being of the whole community than were those of men. "Let her works praise her in the gates!" (Prov. 31:31)—thus concludes the poem in praise of "the valorous woman" of Proverbs. Here Boaz indicates that Ruth's "acts-of-good-faith" to Naomi have been doing just that.

a valorous woman—Having asked Ruth who she is, Boaz here answers his own question: She is a woman whose valor (*ḥayîl*) is manifested in her acts-of-good-faith (*ḥesed*). In naming her "a valorous woman" (alternatively, "a woman of substance"), Boaz unconsciously names her as a match for himself; the phrase is a near echo of the way Boaz is first described (see the note at 2:1). When the word *ḥayîl* is first used of Boaz, it might seem to be nothing more than a statement of his economic status. Yet shortly, he begins to emerge as a man of substantial personal character. In partial contrast to Boaz, Ruth's "substance" is entirely one of character. Nonetheless, as Boaz recognizes, that is more than enough to make her the right match for him. This recognition is already reflected in his statement of assurance to her here. At the very same time that he offers her protection ("Do not be afraid"), he also implicitly accedes to her good judgment ("Everything that you say, I will do"). Thus the narrator shows us the beginning of a relationship in which each partner can rely fully on the other.

A reader familiar with biblical literature may also recognize that the phrase "a valorous woman" appears at one other place in Scripture, namely, Proverbs 31:10–31. That extended poem of a (female) Israelite householder and domestic manager is probably the most unambiguously flattering portrayal of any person in the whole Bible. In the context of the book of Proverbs, "the valorous woman" is the living representation of the divine quality of wisdom, which is the main subject (one might even say the "main character") of Proverbs. In the Hebrew Bible, the book of Ruth follows immediately after Proverbs. That literary order (from which the Christian ordering of the biblical books departs) makes it easy to draw the connection between the young Moabite Ruth and the valorous Israelite in Proverbs, whose wise work and teaching secure the well-being of her family.

12   *And now—while it is true that I am a redeemer, there is a redeemer even closer than I.*

13   *Stay for the night, and in the morning, if he will redeem you—good, let him redeem. And if he does not desire to redeem you, then I myself will redeem you, as God lives! Lie down until the morning."*

14   *And she lay at the place-of-his-feet until the morning, but she arose before a person can recognize his neighbor. For he thought, "Let it not be known that the woman came to the threshing floor."*

15   *And he said, "Hold out the shawl that you have on and grip it firmly." And she gripped it, and he measured six "barleys." And he set it on her, and he went to the city.*

3:14 *For he thought*—In what follows, Boaz speaks *of* Ruth rather than directly to her. Yet Ruth seems to have arisen in response to Boaz's unspoken thought. Perhaps the narrator is suggesting that the pair is already learning to communicate and to give heed to each other with the subtlety and mutual respect that can make a home truly a "resting-place" (see 3:1).

the woman—This is the first time that Ruth is so described—in contrast to earlier identifications, by herself and others, as "worker-girl" (2:6), "daughter" (2:8), "servant-girl" (2:13), "maidservant" (3:9), and, of course, "the Moabite" (1:22; 2:2, 6). Perhaps the change the narrator subtly registers in Boaz's perception of Ruth is another oblique answer to his question, "Who are you?"

3:15 *"barleys"*—The size of the portion is not specified, so it must have been a standard measure. A reasonable guess is the seah, which is one-third of an ephah (2:17). This quantity would weigh at least sixty and possibly as much as one hundred pounds! Is Boaz sending Ruth home to Naomi with something like a bride-price in her shawl? If so, that may help explain the startled question that Naomi poses when Ruth appears at the door.

And he measured six "barleys."
(Ruth 3:15)

16   *And she went to her mother-in-law, and she said, "Who are you, my daughter!?" And she told her everything that the man had done for her.*

17   *And she said, "These six 'barleys' he gave me, for he said, 'Don't go empty to your mother-in-law.'"*

18   *And she said, "Sit down, my daughter, until you know how the matter falls out. For the man will not be quiet until he has completed the matter . . . today!"*

3:16 *Who are you, my daughter!?*—Clearly, literal recognition is not the issue, and Ruth does not answer the question directly (as though she were unrecognizable in the dark). Rather, she tells Naomi what has happened in the hours since she left home—events that have made her, in some sense, unrecognizable to Naomi. Even though she was following the instructions of her mother-in-law, her actions have brought Ruth fully into her independent identity (see the note at 3:9). On the threshing floor, she took the risk of bitter humiliation and loss of reputation. But in so doing, she found the most profound regard; she secured a future for herself and her mother-in-law. Ruth is now a "woman" (3:14) in her own right. The literary art of the author is evident in this third repetition of a question about Ruth's identity (see also 2:5; 3:9). In the previous instances, it was an obvious question to ask, although not without significance (see the note at 3:9). But just because the question is not obvious here, it makes us consider what we now know about who Ruth is. Above all, she is characterized by multiple "acts-of-good-faith" (*ḥesed*). Now that we see her as a woman who is independent, bold, and even physically strong, we can better understand what such "good-faith" means in a human life. It is what binds humans to one another and to God. And in Ruth we see that the perfect practice of *ḥesed* requires strength so that one can bind oneself freely to others—not primarily out of abject need, but out of generous love.

3:17 *empty*—Unconsciously, Boaz echoes Naomi's self-description when she first returned "empty" to Bethlehem (1:21).

And she said, "Who are you, my daughter!?"
(Ruth 3:16)

CHAPTER FOUR

Redeemer

1   Now Boaz went up to the gate and sat there. And here, passing by, is the redeemer of whom Boaz had spoken. And he said to him, "Turn aside, sit here, P'loni Almoni." And he turned aside and sat.

2   And he took ten men from among the elders of the city, and he said, "Sit here," and they sat.

4:1 *And here, passing by, is*—The shift to present tense points to the fact that here, for a second time (see the note at 3:8), the narrator uses a participial clause that seems to give us direct access to Boaz's own perceptions as this moment of opportunity presents itself.

the redeemer—The word occurs twenty times in this and the preceding chapter (3:9, 12, 13; 4:1, 3, 4, 6, 8, 14). As we have seen previously, multiple repetitions of key words (see the notes at 1:6 and 2:2) identify a central theme of this book and, indeed, of the Bible as a whole—namely, redemption of a painful past and a seemingly hopeless present. The past is not erased; notably, the names of all the dead men are remembered in this chapter (see vv. 9–10). Rather, through memory the dead are incorporated into a new and rich life, one that opens into an abundantly promising future.

P'loni Almoni—This is not a real name but rather a rhyming parody, similar to "Joe Schmoe" in English. We can safely assume that Boaz does in fact know the man's name; they are relatives living in the same small town. So why does Boaz address him in a way that seems deliberately demeaning? Rudeness is inconsistent with what we know of Boaz's character and, moreover, of his shrewdness; after all, Boaz's personal happiness depends on the outcome of this meeting. It is likely that Boaz does not actually use this somewhat contemptuous name to his relative's face. Rather, the narrator adds it in order to give us, the audience, a hint of what is to come. When this unnamed person refuses to act as redeemer and marry Ruth, he effectively drops out of history: the family history, and also Israel's history, in which Ruth and her offspring will come to figure prominently. He renders himself, in effect, nameless. Perhaps also the narrator is suggesting that forfeiting the role of redeemer is a contemptible act—even if Boaz is banking on forfeiture. The man who refuses Ruth does not deserve to be remembered by name.

4:2 *and they sat*—The elders respond to Boaz's terse command with the same unquestioning alacrity as does P'loni Almoni himself. Boaz evidently exercises considerable influence within the community.

3   *And he said to the redeemer, "The portion of the field that belonged to our brother, to Elimelekh —Naomi has put it up for sale . . . the one who returned from the field of Moab.*

4   *And now I say (I will uncover your ear): Acquire, before those seated and before the elders of my people! If you are going to act-as-redeemer, then act-as-redeemer. And if you will not act-as-redeemer, then tell me, so I may know. For there is no one except you to act-as-redeemer, and I am after you." And he said, "I will myself act-as-redeemer."*

4:4 *I will uncover your ear*—Now that "the redeemer" has sat down before the quickly assembled council of elders, Boaz opens a formal address, in which he chooses his words carefully. This phrase appears elsewhere to indicate that the speaker is in a position to disclose information that could not come from another source, for example, in King Saul's confiding of his every intention to his son Jonathan (1 Sam. 20:2) or in God's revealing of the divine plan to David (2 Sam. 7:27). Thus Boaz presents himself as someone whose word is worthy of both close attention and trust. In fact, however, Boaz is about to make use of a bait-and-switch ploy that casts the would-be redeemer in an unfavorable public light.

Acquire . . . act-as-redeemer—Somewhat unusually, these verbal forms appear without a direct object; there is no mention of what (or who) is to be acquired or redeemed—the land, or even Ruth. The latter verb commonly occurs with a direct object, for example, "if he will redeem *you*" (3:13). Here the same verb is translated in a different way ("act-as-redeemer"), because the lack of an *object* puts the focus entirely upon the *subject*—that is, the person who will (or will not) enact the role of redeemer. Fivefold repetition of this verb in the verse sharpens that focus on the subject. Furthermore, the fact that "acquire" likewise has no named object will become significant in the following verse, where the object of acquisition appears in an ambiguous light.

5A   *And Boaz said, "On the day of your acquiring the field from the hand of Naomi and*—ahem!—*Ruth the Moabite, wife of the dead,* you *acquire, in order to raise up the name of the dead over his ancestral property."*

5B   *And Boaz said, "On the day of your acquiring the field from the hand of Naomi and*—ahem!—*Ruth the Moabite, wife of the dead,* I *acquire, in order to raise up the name of the dead over his ancestral property."*

5C   *And Boaz said, "On the day of your acquiring the field from the hand of Naomi* and from *Ruth the Moabite, wife of the dead,* you *acquire, in order to raise up the name of the dead over his ancestral property."*

4:5 The Hebrew text for this verse is grammatically difficult and ambiguous at two points. First, before naming Ruth, Boaz inserts a grammatical particle whose meaning is hard to identify. It might sound to his listeners something like a throat-clearing (*"ahem!"*). Second, the Hebrew scribal tradition preserves two alternative readings for one word: "you acquire" or "I acquire." Therefore, no single translation can convey the multiple interpretive possibilities that the Hebrew allows.

Yet it is probably no coincidence that this is the one truly problematic verse in a story that is otherwise told in a simple style. Slowing down at this point to ponder various possibilities serves two positive functions. First, it heightens suspense: this is the point where the drama and uncertainty of the women's lives (and now Boaz's life as well) come to a head. Second, if the reader is not quite sure what Boaz means to say, perhaps that is because he is deliberately befuddling his immediate audience, namely, P'loni Almoni—and maybe even the elders whom he has assembled to judge the case. Because the textual difficulty here is assumed to be purposeful, three different translations are offered.

All three interpretive options indicate that Boaz is now switching the terms of the agreement to which the prospective redeemer has committed himself. He is indeed "uncovering the ear," revealing a new piece of information that P'loni Almoni cannot have foreseen. Ruth was not previously mentioned with respect to the land sale (v. 3), but now Boaz inserts her into the deal with the most striking description possible: "Ruth the Moabite, wife of the dead." Perhaps he is evoking the plight of the childless sojourner in order to appeal to the sympathy of his audience of elders. Or perhaps Boaz is deliberately presenting her in the objectivizing terms that will be *least* appealing to his rival "redeemer." At any rate, mention of her in this context changes things completely. Suddenly, the financial gain that P'loni Almoni might have expected evaporates before his eyes. He might have hoped to enlarge his own landholding for himself and his descendents. But now Boaz insists that the ancestral property Naomi has put up for sale is to remain associated with the name of "the dead"—namely, Elimelekh and his son Maḥlon, who still has some claim as Ruth's husband.

This is a "switch" of real magnitude. No longer is the issue merely keeping the property of an indigent relative within the extended family (the ordinary scope of a redeemer's responsibility). Boaz now implicitly adds the further responsibility of raising up a son for the men who have no living descendants, of perpetuating the names of those who are in danger of being erased from all memory. This would have been perceived as the greatest tragedy that could befall a person, for through most of the biblical period, Israel had no conviction that life continued after death. (The three Abrahamic faiths—Judaism, Christianity, and Islam—have all moved beyond ancient Israel in affirming belief in life after death.) The Israelites thought that a person "lived" after death only in a derivative sense, through descendants living on the ancestral land and worshiping the God of "Abraham, Isaac, and Jacob," the ancestors of all Israel.

In all three possible renderings, the ultimate goal is "to raise up the name of the dead over his ancestral property." In other words, Boaz insists that Ruth is to enter into a kind of marriage, practiced in ancient Israel and some other traditional societies, known as levirate marriage. By this practice, a childless widow might marry a brother-in-law living in the same family compound (Deut. 25:5–6). The intended advantages were twofold. First, such an arrangement would offer protection and support to a woman who was no longer virgin and therefore not easily marriageable; her life would continue in the same family she had joined in her first marriage. Second, it would provide "issue" for the dead brother. The first son of the new marriage would be counted as his, "so that his name might not be erased from Israel" (Deut. 25:6; cf. Ruth 4:10).

P'loni Almoni is understandably taken aback by the switch, for the custom normally obtained only between two full brothers who had been living in the same compound. P'loni Almoni is probably no closer than a cousin to the dead men, and Boaz is even further removed. But Boaz, perhaps to tighten the screw, now refers to "our brother, to Elimelekh" (4:3). We have already seen that Boaz's authority at the gate is unquestioned. P'loni Almoni evidently sees no possibility of challenging his interpretation of the legal situation. And so he backs out, as Boaz expects him to do, for reasons that become clear in the next verse.

On these basic points all three renderings of the verse are in agreement. But they differ in the kind of authority Boaz wields, and also in how he represents Ruth. Translations A and B differ in the subject of the verb "acquire." In Translation A, Boaz boldly pronounces P'loni Almoni's legal obligation to take Ruth along with the field but reminds him that the field will be his only until the son Ruth bears attains majority. In Translation B, he asserts a more subtle form of authority, namely, that of moral superiority. P'loni Almoni may take the land, but Boaz will take Ruth, care for her, and sire and raise a boy who will one day grow up to take over the field in the name of the dead. And he will do all this even without the temporary gain of a productive field. In Translation C, no man "acquires" Ruth. She is represented, with great respect, as co-owner of the land, alongside

Naomi; she is an independent agent who has the right to sell her property. Nonetheless, the sale will not be permanent: Boaz reminds P'loni Almoni that if he acquires the field, he ultimately does so only to tend it until Ruth raises a son to reclaim it.

Probably, those who preserved the Hebrew text saw some value in each of these interpretations, and so, in the complicated structure and wording of this verse, they have preserved all three of them.

6   *And the redeemer said, "I cannot act-as-redeemer myself, lest I destroy my own ancestral property. So now you, redeem for yourself my right-of-redemption, for I cannot act-as-redeemer."*

7   *Thus it was formerly in Israel concerning the right-of-redemption and concerning exchange, in order to validate any legal matter: A man removed his sandal and gave it to his fellow. And this was the manner of attestation in Israel.*

8   *And the redeemer said to Boaz, "Acquire for yourself." And he removed his sandal.*

4:6 *lest I destroy my own ancestral property*—The term "destroy" is a strong one; P'loni Almoni now views the prospect with some horror. At the least (that is, even if Ruth marries Boaz), he stands to invest in a piece of property that will eventually revert to Ruth's grown son, presumably without reimbursement for the "redeemer." If P'loni Almoni himself "acquires" Ruth, then he will make an even heavier investment, in feeding Ruth, Naomi, and a child who will count as another man's heir. Few Israelite farmers had the means to take on a second family. It is likely that P'loni Almoni is already married, or at least wishes to marry and have offspring. He cannot afford to divide his small resources in this way. Maybe the deal is further undesirable to him because, as Boaz stresses, Ruth is not only "the wife of the dead" but also "the Moabite" (v. 5). At any rate, P'loni Almoni, like Orpah (1:14), chooses the course of expediency and ordinary caution.

4:8 *he removed his sandal*—The custom is not well understood, and this was probably true even in ancient times, since the narrator—or a later editor—makes a rare aside (v. 7) in order to offer some slight explanation. We can only guess why the symbol of the sandal figures in the transfer of land: perhaps the right to "walk off" the boundaries of this plot, marking it as one's own? An Israelite poet imaginatively portrays God thus laying claim to a whole country: "On Edom I cast my sandal" (Ps. 60:10 Heb. [8 Eng.]). Further, it is not even clear whose sandal is removed, and by whom: Boaz or the redeemer. The narrator seems content to leave the details uncertain, and maybe that is because the precise function of the sandal in this antiquated legal practice is not important.

However, there is one biblical context in which removing a sandal is a well-understood gesture—that is, in the case of a man who refuses to enter into a levirate marriage with his widowed sister-in-law. Then the jilted woman may publicly humiliate him by taking off his sandal and spitting in his face (Deut. 25:7–10). It is likely that the narrator intends for us to recall that situation of humiliation here. Ruth is not a typical candidate for levirate marriage, and the narrator stops short of having her remove P'loni Almoni's sandal or spit in his face. But Boaz has insisted that Ruth and her yet-to-be-conceived son are entitled to something of the protection that levirate marriage provides, and P'loni Almoni has declined to become involved. Having evoked the custom of levirate marriage, the narrator now evokes the further symbol of the sandal. The combined effect is that the would-be redeemer seems to condemn himself, even though no one speaks against him.

And the redeemer said to Boaz, "Acquire for yourself."
And he removed his sandal.
(Ruth 4:8)

9 *And Boaz said to the elders and all the people, "You are witnesses this day that I have acquired everything that was Elimelekh's, and everything that was Kilyon's and Maḥlon's, from the hand of Naomi.*

10 *And also Ruth the Moabite, the wife of Maḥlon, I have acquired for my own wife, in order to raise up the name of the dead over his ancestral property, that the name of the dead may not be cut off from his kin and from the gate of his home-place. You are witnesses this day."*

11 *And all the people who were at the gate and the elders said, "Witnesses! May YHWH grant that the woman coming into your house be like Rachel and like Leah — the two of whom built up the house of Israel!*

  Now, do valorously in Ephratah,

  And proclaim a name in Bethlehem!

4:10 *from his kin and from the gate of his home-place*—The phrasing points to the fact that an Israelite's identity was bound up with a "home-place" (as many rural English speakers still say) as much as with family. To die and be buried away from home was a tragedy. This strong sense of belonging to a place persists in the modern Middle East, at least among those still living in traditional cultures, and it figures importantly in the consciousness of those who have been forcibly displaced (by political and military action or by economic constraints) from their ancestral homes.

4:11 *Witnesses!*—Oddly to us, biblical Hebrew does not have a word for "yes." The response of agreement echoes the significant word in the original statement.

May YHWH grant that the woman coming into your house be like Rachel and like Leah—The two wives of Jacob/Israel, the ancestor for whom the whole people is named, competed fiercely to produce twelve sons—and one daughter (Gen. 29:31–30:24). While the competition created a sadness in the lives of the two women, themselves sisters, its fruit is recognized as a blessing in later generations. To this day, Orthodox Jewish parents say this Sabbath blessing over their young daughters: "May God make you like Sarah, Rebecca, Rachel, and Leah." Most noteworthy is the fact that, in the eyes of the people at the gate, Ruth has ceased to be "the Moabite." This blessing marks her as fully integrated into her adopted community; she is now an Israelite woman.

do valorously—The last two lines have a poetic rhythm and may be a standard blessing offered to a groom. The word rendered here "valorously" (*ḥayîl*) may indicate material wealth (see the note at 2:1). We might suppose that in conventional usage, a groom would be wished material prosperity, and that may be how the blessing was commonly understood. But in the context of this book, the word, applied to both Boaz and Ruth, connotes the richness, or "substance," of their personal characters (see the notes at 2:1 and 3:11). So it is most likely that we are to hear the blessing as a prayer that this couple may continue and even increase acts of "valor" in their life together and may pass that distinctive character on to their children and descendants.

proclaim a name—There is a pleasing irony here for those who know the larger story of Israel. Boaz has pledged through this marriage to perpetuate the name of the dead in Bethlehem. But in fact, it is the names of the living and not-yet-born that will be widely proclaimed and remembered as a result of this marriage—starting with Boaz's own name, and Ruth's, which will go down in Israelite history and be remembered through all ages (see the genealogy in Matt. 1:5; cf. Luke 3:32). Much more widely proclaimed are the names of two children who issue from the line now established: King David and (in New Testament tradition) Jesus. However, it should not be overlooked that the very first name to be joyfully proclaimed in connection with this new marriage is the name of YHWH (v. 14). Although this narrative says little directly about God, one might read here a message congenial with that of the psalmist's teaching:

> If YHWH does not build a house,
>> then its builders strive at it in vain.
>>> (Ps. 127:1)

And Boaz said to the elders and all the people,
"You are witnesses this day."
(Ruth 4:9)

12   *And may your house be like the house of Peretz whom Tamar bore to Judah, from the seed that YHWH gives to you, from this worker-girl!"*

13   *And Boaz took Ruth, and she became his wife, and he went to her, and YHWH gave her pregnancy, and she bore a son.*

14   *And the women said to Naomi, "Blessed is YHWH, who has not allowed a redeemer to cease for you this day! And may his name be proclaimed in Israel!*

4:12 *Peretz whom Tamar bore to Judah*—Peretz is nothing more than a biblical name with no personal history attached. He is important only as a part of the line that connects Boaz to Judah, one of Jacob's twelve sons, and the one for whom the most important of the twelve tribes is named. Doubtless, one reason Peretz is mentioned is for the sake of his mother, Tamar. It is significant that Tamar is evoked now, at the end of the story, just before Ruth is named for the last time. For in recalling the story of the ancestress renowned for her boldness (Gen. 38), we understand better how Ruth is truly "a woman of valor." Like Tamar, she takes the risk of being sexually aggressive in a culture that denies that role to women, and she does it in order to secure her own future. Moreover, like Tamar, Ruth makes a permanent contribution to the future of the people precisely through her multidimensional sexual role: as wife, as mother, and as ancestress to the kings of Israel. It is a striking thing that Tamar and Ruth are two of the four Israelite women whom the evangelist Matthew mentions alongside Mary in the long genealogy that opens his Gospel (Matt. 1:2–16). They anticipate Mary's role as a mother. Each of them serves God most fully by allowing her body to be a vehicle for the fulfillment of God's plan in history. If now we see clearly who Ruth is, we see her also for the last time. Once the child is born (v. 13), she disappears from view.

4:13 *and YHWH gave her pregnancy*—This stands out as one of only two direct statements from the narrator about God's action (cf. 1:6). Thus it underscores the fact that the child's birth is a providential event, the blessed result of both extraordinary human actions and the common but never less-than-miraculous action of God in making the womb fruitful.

4:14 *who has not allowed a redeemer to cease for you*—The peculiarity of this phrase is to be taken seriously as a clue to meaning. It seems that YHWH is here blessed as the Source of a steady stream of redeemers! And indeed, more than one redeemer is indicated. We have already seen Boaz act as redeemer, but here the women seem to be thinking above all of the unborn child (see v. 15). In him, Naomi will find personal "redemption," that is, a secure old age (v. 15), supported by the boy who supplies the place of the sons she bore from her own body (see v. 16). Further, the perpetuation of a redeemer portends a larger future, as the following genealogy shows. The child to be born is the grandfather of David, and it is from his royal house that, as both Jews and Christians attest, the messianic Redeemer of all Israel will come (for Jews) or has come (for Christians). So this marriage and the family that Ruth and Boaz now form are important for the whole salvation history of Israel.

And Boaz took Ruth, and she became his wife.
(Ruth 4:13)

15   *And may he be to you as one who restores life and sup-ports your gray-headed-years. For your bride-daughter who loves you has borne him —she who is better to you than seven sons!"*

16   *And Naomi took the child and held him to her body, and she became his nursemaid.*

17   *And the neighbor-women gave him a name, saying, "A son is born to Naomi," and they named him Obed. He is the father of Jesse, the father of David.*

4:15 *one who restores life*—As noted above, the one who is to restore Naomi's life is the boy Obed. At the same time, it is striking that this phrase appears only one other time in the Bible, and in that case it refers to Israel's great Redeemer, YHWH:

> YHWH is my shepherd; I shall not lack.
> > In grassy pastures he causes me to lie down.
> Beside restful waters he leads me.
> > He restores my life.
>
> (Ps. 23:1–3)

So this phrase would seem to be another case in which, through the vehicle of language, the human redeemer becomes transparent to the action of God.

4:17 *A son is born to Naomi*—The book ends in a way that we do not expect. Boaz and our heroine Ruth are gone from sight, a clear indication that this book is finally something other than a romance. In the end, only the old woman is left, holding the child who is her future and that of her people. It is a picture of complete personal restoration, against all odds. She who walked away "full" (with husband and children), even in the midst of famine, and returned empty (1:21) is now full again in the most palpable sense, holding the living child to her body.

The fact that Ruth's child is said to be "born to Naomi" is the most remarkable statement in the entire book about the relationship between the two women. Ruth once took it upon herself to share fully the unpromising future of the empty old woman; as a result, Naomi is now granted the full measure of Ruth's fruitfulness. Yet there is restoration and gain also on Ruth's side of the partnership. For it is through Naomi that Ruth ceases to be the noteworthy and even suspicious "Moabite woman," the stranger in a small town. The fact that Ruth is now not named may simply indicate how fully she has been assimilated, in the public mind, into Naomi's Israelite family, whose story is now unfolding in a new generation. For the one who has suffered as a foreigner, there can be no greater assurance than to find herself blending in unnoticeably.

Obed—The name means "one who serves." It may be a prayer that the child's life be dedicated to the service of God, but it is also a reminder that his life is dedicated to the care of the "mother" who holds him.

And Naomi took the child and held him to her body.
(Ruth 4:16)

18   *These are the generations of Peretz: Peretz sired Hetzron.*

19   *And Hetzron sired Ram, and Ram sired Ammi-nadav.*

20   *And Ammi-nadav sired Naḥshon, and Naḥshon sired Salmah.*

4:18 *These are the generations of Peretz*—The circle has been completed for Naomi. And at the last, through the genealogy, the circle opens up toward the future of the people Israel. Genealogies are for most modern readers the least meaningful parts of the biblical text, but it would be hard to overestimate their importance for a traditional culture such as ancient Israel. They encode essential historical, cultural, and personal information in the most "portable"—that is, easily memorized—form. One might ask why this genealogy begins with Peretz; one reason (his mother Tamar) has already been noted. But this in itself seems an insufficient reason to repeat the name of an otherwise nonfunctional ancestor. Why not begin with someone more important, like Peretz's father, Judah, or Abraham himself?

Maybe the key thing to notice here is that the genealogical distance from Peretz to David is exactly ten generations. Ten generations is a significant span in biblical genealogies. The very first genealogies—Adam to Noah (Gen. 5) and Shem to Abraham (Gen. 11)—are also ten generations in length. More importantly, they demonstrate the same pattern as this genealogy, reaching a climactic point in the tenth generation. Noah, Abraham, and David—each of these "tenth men" is privileged to enter into a new covenant with God on behalf of humankind or Israel in particular. And each covenant signals a fresh and redemptive beginning after a long period of history marked by human violence.

Moreover, the span of ten generations is crucial with respect to an issue that figures prominently in this book, namely, the status of Moabites in Israel. According to Deuteronomy, the descendent of a hostile nation, an Ammonite or Moabite, is prohibited from entering the congregation of Israel "even to the tenth generation" (Deut. 23:4 Heb. [3 Eng.]). Perhaps David's Moabite great-grandmother was a scandal in Israel. But on his father's side, Peretz was also the son of a foreign woman, Tamar the Canaanite. So maybe the genealogy is offering a kind of "homeopathic" remedy for the scandal of foreign blood—that is, it heals by applying more of the same. Subtly, it suggests that the ten-generation prohibition has reached its terminus in David. It is time to welcome the outsider.

21   *And Salmon (Salmah) sired Boaz, and Boaz sired Obed.*

22   *And Obed sired Jesse, and Jesse sired David.*

4:22 *David*—In this book about common folk of extraordinary character, the (literally) last word belongs to the great king who is their descendant. An ancient rabbinic teaching enables us to see that this name is, in effect, a climactic statement on the "valorous" characters of Boaz and Ruth (see the notes at 2:1, 3:11, and 4:11): "Rabbi Abbahu said: If a giant marries a giantess, what do they produce? Mighty men. Boaz married Ruth. Whom did they produce? David, of whom it is said, '. . . skillful in playing, a mighty man of valor . . .' [1 Sam 16:18]" (*Midrash Rabbah* to Ruth 2:1).

And Boaz sired Obed. And Obed sired Jesse, and Jesse sired David.
(Ruth 4:21–22)

Works Cited

Carlisle, Thomas John. *Eve and After: Old Testament Women in Portrait*. Grand Rapids: Wm. B. Eerdmans, 1984.

Childs, Brevard. "The Genre of Biblical Commentary as Problem and Challenge." In *Tehillah le-Moshe: Biblical and Judaic Studies in Honor of Moshe Greenberg*, ed. Mordechai Cogan, Barry L. Eichler, and Jeffrey H. Tigay, 185–92. Winona Lake, Ind.: Eisenbrauns, 1997.

Davis, Ellen F. *Proverbs, Ecclesiastes, and the Song of Songs*. Louisville, Ky.: Westminster John Knox, 2000.

Elmendorf, Dwight L. *A Camera Crusade through the Holy Land*. New York: Scribner, 1912.

Knox, Ronald. *On Englishing the Bible*. London: Burns Oates, 1949.

Matisse, Henri. "Looking at Life with the Eyes of a Child." In *Matisse on Art*, ed. Jack D. Flam, 148–49. New York: E. P. Dutton, 1978.

Neusner, Jacob. *The Mother of the Messiah in Judaism: The Book of Ruth*. Valley Forge, Pa.: Trinity Press International, 1993.

Rabinowitz, L., trans. *Midrash Rabbah*. Ed. H. Freedman and Maurice Simon. Vol. 8. London: The Soncino Press, 1939.

Sasson, Jack M. *Ruth: A New Translation with a Philological Commentary and a Formalist-Folklorist Interpretation*. Baltimore: Johns Hopkins University Press, 1979.